THE VEGETABLE GARDEN

The well-balanced kitchen garden in a setting reasonably ornamental need not be the proverbial "eyesore" of years gone by

The Garden Library

THE VEGETABLE GARDEN

REVISED AND ENLARGED

BY
ADOLPH KRUHM

FROM THE ORIGINAL TEXT
OF
I. D. BENNETT

PUBLISHED BY
DOUBLEDAY, DORAN & COMPANY, INC.
FOR
THE NATIONAL GARDEN ASSOCIATION
1928

COPYRIGHT, 1908, 1923, BY
DOUBLEDAY, PAGE & COMPANY

ALL RIGHTS RESERVED, INCLUDING THAT OF TRANSLATION
INTO FOREIGN LANGUAGES, INCLUDING THE SCANDINAVIAN

PRINTED IN THE UNITED STATES
AT
THE COUNTRY LIFE PRESS, GARDEN CITY, N. Y.

A NOTE

IN BRINGING the text of this edition up to date the material on vegetables and their culture by Mr. Kruhm, published in *The Garden Magazine* during the past few years, has been freely drawn upon to make the present volume well balanced with worthwhile up-to-date information.

Acknowledgments for special contributions in the original text are made to Dr. E. Porter Felt and William C. McCollom in the preparation of the chapter on Spraying; to Parker Thayer Barnes in the preparation of the chapter on Fertilizing and parts of the chapter on Garden Tools.

CONTENTS

CHAPTER		PAGE
I.	THE ECONOMIC VALUE OF THE KITCHEN GARDEN	1
II.	DETERMINING WHAT'S REALLY WANTED	5
III.	THE LOCATION OF THE GARDEN	10
IV.	PLANNING THE GARDEN	15
V.	HOW TO MAINTAIN FERTILITY	21
VI.	ON THE SOWING OF SEED	39
VII.	TRANSPLANTING	44
VIII.	INTENSIVE CULTIVATION AND ITS PRACTICE	56
IX.	TOOLS WHICH MAKE GARDENING EASY	60
X.	ON THE GROWING OF VARIOUS VEGETABLES	71
XI.	ROOT VEGETABLES	97
XII.	VINE VEGETABLES AND FRUITS	123
XIII.	GREENS AND SALAD VEGETABLES	136
XIV.	PERENNIAL VEGETABLES	154
XV.	THE MIDSUMMER GARDEN	166
XVI.	STORING VEGETABLES IN WINTER	172
XVII.	THE CONSTRUCTION AND CARE OF HOTBEDS, COLDFRAMES, AND PITS	179
XVIII.	THE GARDEN'S ENEMIES	207
XIX.	FALL WORK IN THE GARDEN	220
	INDEX	229

LIST OF ILLUSTRATIONS

The well balanced kitchen garden, in a setting reasonably ornamental need not be the proverbial "eyesore" of years gone by . . *Frontispiece*	
	FACING PAGE
This leaves room for several rows of fruit and a generous asparagus bed in the rear	20
Liquid manure is one of the best acting fertilisers	21
Deep digging, frequent manuring and an occasional application of lime are essential to maintain a high degree of fertility	36
Cultivation is fertilisation in that air and oxygen are just as essential to good crops as potash, phosphates, etc.	37
Paper collar to protect plant from cut worms .	52
A home-made dibble	52
A good type of seed flat in which a small number of seedlings are readily raised	52
Keep records of all work done, in both book and in form of garden labels carrying variety names and planting dates.	53
A fine example of intensive cultivation showing young lettuce between tomatoes.	53

ILLUSTRATIONS

FACING PAGE

The modern wheelhoe is now indispensable in even the small garden. The two wheel type shown here is considered the most practical . . .   68

The power tool for the garden has come to stay. About a dozen kinds and models compete for the user's favour   68

For heavy clay soils, the tooth-type of hand cultivator is best. (Liberty type shown here). .   69

The modern adaptation of the old Dutch scuffle hoe, the Gilson weeder which is the tool "par excellence" to kill surface weeds on light soils.   69

Two never-failing quality kinds, Golden Bantam and White Evergreen, the finest type of ever popular Stowell's Evergreen   84

Well grown cabbage is quite an ornamental feature of the kitchen garden. Surehead, shown here, is the best all-round strain of Premium Flat Dutch type   85

The well balanced kitchen garden invariably holds an abundance of root crops which fortify the home against want of vitamines during the winter   100

Onions, such as these Yellow Globe Danvers, are easily grown from seeds in 100 days. Text tells how   101

The methods by which such "hills" of five-pound crops as shown above, are grown, are fully described in accompanying chapters   116

[x]

ILLUSTRATIONS

FACING PAGE

Crisp, brittle delicacies that make your mouth water, are easily grown in even smallest gardens   **117**

The White Spine type of cucumbers provides fruits for both slicing and pickles. Early White Spine shown here **132**

The fruit that made Rocky Ford famous from coast to coast and that helped to extend melon culture considerably **133**

Nothing comes up to the "Butter-head" type in quality and among them Wayahead is way ahead in every respect **148**

The Chinese have sent us many queer things, but the usefulness of Chinese cabbage as a salad has been firmly established **149**

The well-stocked midsummer garden holds an abundance of every kind of vegetable. Tomatoes, Swiss chard and beans shown here. .   **164**

Carrots easily rank among the most profitable root crops, while their foliage is quite ornamental. Variety Amsterdam Forcing shown here is one of the best for early outdoor work .   **165**

The well-stocked frame serves as insurance for early crops and against late frosts **180**

Straw mat for use in very cold weather . . .   **181**

To get the most out of every tomato plant, it should be staked and pruned. The waste due to growing crop on the ground runs as high as 30 per cent. **196**

[xi]

ILLUSTRATIONS

FACING PAGE

This shows the "suckers" that thrive at the expense of the clusters, on every plant. Remove them at the leaf joints, throughout the season   197

There is no use making a garden unless you propose to defend it against its enemies. The Knapsack type of sprayer works well in large gardens. The small gardener will be delighted with the handy type of Aerospra, Jr. . . .   212

Don't let the leaf chewing insects feast at your expense. Paris green or slugshot are good remedies to keep on hand. The handy duster makes the work a pleasure   213

THE VEGETABLE GARDEN

THE VEGETABLE GARDEN

CHAPTER ONE
THE ECONOMIC VALUE OF THE KITCHEN GARDEN

THE last decade has seen America make rapid strides in a deeper appreciation of the home vegetable garden. People have always appreciated the importance of a proper diet, in which vegetables play a significant rôle, and scientific discovery made during recent years have but strengthened the position of vegetables as bearers of the elusive Vitamines, with the result that vegetables are now looked upon as being of far greater importance than many heavier and richer foods.

There is really only one way in which one may enjoy strictly fresh vegetables and that is to grow them right at the back door, so to say. The process of deterioration due to shipment or transportation to market is great with all vegetables but

THE VEGETABLE GARDEN

especially with those that home gardeners prize most. Corn, peas, lettuce, rapidly change from delicious delicacies to tasteless pulp after becoming hardened or wilted. However, this is but one of the minor reasons why we should take increased interest in the home vegetable garden. Quality vegetables such as are truly appreciated on the home table are rarely ever available in the market. The reasons for this are two-fold:

The commercial grower grows vegetables for their looks and lasting qualities. The lasting quality in vegetable means fibre. Beans, that look well on the market bench after being displayed for several hours, must of necessity contain plenty of fibre; the brittle stringless bush beans gathered in one's own garden would wilt within a very few hours and their appearance would make them unsaleable.

There is another point that has weight with the careful housewife—that of perfect cleanliness. If vegetables look clean and fresh one is apt to infer that they are fresh from the garden. This may be anything but the case. Market gardeners are not independent of time and seasons any more than the rest of mankind, and often find their crop

VALUE OF THE KITCHEN GARDEN

ripening in advance of the market; especially is this the case in small cities or country towns, and the vegetables bought as fresh may have lain in the cellar of the gardener or green grocer for a week or more, and finally been sorted out from a heap of decaying matter and given a bath to make them presentable for offering for sale.

Much of the garden stuff offered in the open market or peddled from door to door was gathered the day before or even earlier and hauled long distances in an uncovered wagon over a dusty road, and we all know of what the dust of the road is composed, afterwards to lie exhibited on open stalls in markets or in front of stores, exposed to the flies or the attentions of every passing dog—and the benches are seldom above high-water mark—and the unspeakable dust and filth of the streets.

All this bids one pause when tempted to order one's daily supply of fresh vegetables from one's local grocer. Certainly it should, if one has a bit of land at command and the strength and ambition to work it or even the will to hire it worked, for there is profit, real and realisable profit, in the growing of one's own vegetables. Profit of health and of pocket for the expense of a small kitchen

THE VEGETABLE GARDEN

garden, properly managed, is light, the returns certain and enjoyable.

There are no vegetables like those which come wet with the morning dew from one's own garden to grace the breakfast table with the toothsome crispness of the scarlet radish or the fresh coolness of lettuce. Sweet corn, when detached from the parent stalk and has felt the heat of the day, loses half its sweetness; and peas have a delicate flavour easily impaired by lying in heaps, even though in a cool place.

To my mind there is nothing more disheartening on a marketing expedition than the sight of the limp vegetables exposed for sale, and it must indeed be a dearth in the family larder which induces me to purchase.

As to the expense incurred in growing one's own vegetables, it will be found comprised for the main part in the fitting of the land for planting and the trifling outlay for seeds. All varieties of seed, with the exception of peas, are of small cost. The usual five- or ten-cent packets of most kinds will be found ample.

CHAPTER TWO
WHAT IS REALLY WANTED

IN OFFERING specific suggestions as to how to conduct the vegetable garden for satisfactory returns, I am largely governed by the law of averages in likes and dislikes of specific vegetables; also I am assuming that fairly normal soil and weather conditions prevail.

In appraising likes and dislikes, I want to go on record as believing that the last ten years have seen a complete readjustment of ideas regarding the value and usefulness of certain vegetables. Ten years ago, lettuce was looked upon merely as a garnishing for salads and to make dishes look pretty. To-day we know that it brings to our table an element more necessary to our physical welfare than either protein, fat, or carbohydrates, in that it supplies us with the essential vitamines. The same may be said of tomatoes and summer squash, two utterly unrelated vegetable crops, yet carrying

THE VEGETABLE GARDEN

the same beneficial elements so important to the human system.

THE FACTORS THAT REALLY GOVERN

Some vegetables will not thrive in cool soil and seasons, no matter what is done to encourage them; others will not do well with the arrival of warm days, no matter how good the soil nor how thorough the culture; still others will just take their own time about getting ready, regardless of soil, season, weather or anything—so there you are! The crux of the situation is a correct understanding of the different vegetables as individuals that are governed just as much by likes and dislikes, environment, heredity, etc., as human plants! And let it be said here that some of our thoroughbred vegetable varieties are more dependable than some humans!

Consequently, make up your mind *what* you want and *when* you want it and then study if the thing can be done! For instance, no matter what you do or plant, you cannot hope to gather a fine crop of peas in this country during the month of August. Peas are distinctly a cool season crop, so do not waste soil, time, and seeds attempting the

WHAT IS REALLY WANTED

impossible. Analyzing vegetables, as classes, in that light, we have:

    A—The Short Season, Cool Season Crops
    B—The Quick Growing, All Season Crops
    C—The Slow Growing, Long Season Crops
    D—The All Season Crops (of Minor Importance)

Personal dislikes, or lack of space, or lesser usefulness will, in nine cases out of ten, cause egg plants, peppers, melons and pumpkins as well as parsnip and salsify to be classed in group D. Unless you positively prefer them to vegetables more important from a nutritive standpoint, and unless you have the correct soil and climatic conditions, waste no time on them within the limitations of half an acre. The possible exception to this is the pepper of which a few dozen plants will provide an abundance of fruits useful for seasoning or stuffing.

THE SHORT SEASON CROPS OF CLASS A

These embrace the vegetables of which complete sowings should be made of varieties maturing in rapid succession or repeated sowings of kinds becoming ready quickly. Peas, spinach, mustard, and endive will not do their best after the ther-

THE VEGETABLE GARDEN

mometer begins to register 75° to 80° between 11 A. M. and 3 P. M. To get the most out of spinach, mustard and endive, sow them frequently in quantities just large enough to meet your needs. All three make delicious greens either separately or mixed.

THE QUICK GROWING ALL SEASON CROPS, CLASS B

Two possibilities are here offered:—(1) they may be planted in a large number of varieties becoming ready in succession; or (2) successive plantings of one sort may be made. In the case of beets, carrots, kohlrabi and summer squash successive sowings of a limited number of varieties or even of one and the same kind is perfectly satisfactory. Beans, corn, lettuce, and radishes will require at least several varieties; in the case of lettuce and radishes as many varieties as are demanded by the length of the season during which you wish to enjoy them. Radishes and lettuce varieties that thrive in June are utterly useless during July, and those that do well in July will fail utterly during August. In the recommendations of specific varieties named below, you will

WHAT IS REALLY WANTED

find guiding notes that will help solve this problem.

THE SLOW GROWING LONG SEASON CROPS, CLASS C

There is really no problem at all with the long season crops since the seeds must be started early in the spring or they will not yield any crops. The exception to this we find in the cabbage family embracing brussels-sprouts, cauliflower, kale, and common cabbage, all of which may be grown either as an early spring or late fall crop. With onions it is best to sow one kind for early use, one for the principal supply, and one of superior keeping quality. Tomatoes are best grown in several kinds, maturing in succession. Thus, when Bonny Best becomes exhausted, Globe is at its best; and when Globe reaches the zenith of its usefulness Stone and Matchless save the day. Swiss chard and New Zealand spinach continue the supply of greens when spinach and mustard go on a strike because of hot weather.

CHAPTER THREE
THE LOCATION OF THE GARDEN

This is a point which admits of little discussion or advice, as, in the majority of cases, circumstances decide it arbitrarily. Especially is this the case where the only land at command is comprised in the narrow confines of a city back yard or the somewhat more generous area of a suburban lot.

But in the country, where land is abundant, the only restrictive condition is that it should be near the house, so that it may be easily worked and cared for, especially if much of this care must devolve upon the women of the family, as is often the case on the farm. Given here a measure of choice of location, it will be well to select a bit of land well drained and exposed to the sunshine the greater part of the day. The near presence of trees is to be avoided, as these not only furnish more shade than is desirable, but the roots—which extend in all directions over an area equal to the spread

THE LOCATION OF THE GARDEN

of tops—drain all the moisture and much of the nourishment from the soil, much to the detriment of any crop which may be planted in their immediate vicinity.

Low, wet land should be avoided unless it can be thoroughly drained, in which case it often makes excellent garden land.

Clay land does not make an ideal garden soil. A good warm loam, well overlaid with humus—decayed vegetable matter—is the best soil in which to grow garden stuff, but a stiff clay soil may be made to produce good results by heavy manuring and underdraining, but will not warrant the expense if other and better soil is available. The point to be considered in selecting garden soil is to choose that which will grow the greatest variety of vegetables with the least expenditure of labour and fertilizers. There are very few vegetables but what may be grown to a point of perfection satisfactory for the home garden, though they might not produce in quantities to make them remunerative for a market garden where much more is expected of the soil than in private places. Certain soils, like well-drained marsh lands, are ideal for certain vegetables, such as celery, cabbage, etc.

THE VEGETABLE GARDEN

On the small village lot one must, perforce, take what one has, and it is doubtful if there is any bit of land but what may be made, under careful management, to produce a fair amount of vegetation. The fertility of a small area of land is so easily increased that no plot of land need be considered hopeless on that score.

There is one condition to be considered, however, in this method of restoring the soil, and that is the grade. If this is high enough to allow of the removal of any considerable amount of earth, well and good, but if not, fresh earth must be brought in to take its place. However, the ploughing and fertilizing of the soil will raise the grade considerably, and land that at first may appear too low will, in the course of two or three years' cultivation, have quite recovered its usual grade.

It has been said that the near presence of trees is to be avoided in the garden, but the comfort and convenience of working it will be greatly enhanced by the presence of a shed or other building on the north side, where one can store the necessary tools, do much of the indoor work connected with gardening, cleaning vegetables, and the like, or take shelter in a sudden shower. Such a building will

THE LOCATION OF THE GARDEN

afford a suitable location for the construction of hotbeds and coldframes, as well as affording temporary quarters for vegetables, which may need to be gathered in advance of a sudden cold snap. It will also be found invaluable for drying and ripening off such vegetables as are to be stored in the cellar for winter use. A scaffolding of lath, erected just out of the way of one's head, will be found invaluable for drying onions, and will double the capacity of the shed.

Another feature of moment in the selection of a garden site is the nearness and availability of the water supply. Where one has city water the problem is simple—the water may be carried to the garden; but where this does not exist the garden must be carried to the well or a home system of water established. This may be accomplished satisfactorily by the erection of a wind-mill operated through a three-way pump, which will convey water to any point in the ground. Even the mill may be dispensed with and water carried to a stand pipe supplied with a hose and nozzle, whence it may be distributed about the garden as needed. It is necessary, however, in installing a force pump of any make to know just what you are getting, and not find one's self encumbered with a pump which it is a punishment to work or one with insufficient force to throw a reasonable stream of water.

The presence of a shed and a water supply adjacent will be found of the greatest convenience to the housewife, who can there prepare the vegetables for the table, doing away with much dirt about the kitchen and the subsequent disposal of the tops, husks, and other refuse.

CHAPTER FOUR
PLANNING THE GARDEN

The work of planning the garden—inasmuch as it consists in deciding what and how much we shall plant and where we shall plant it—may very well be done long in advance of the season of active operations. Indeed, it is a distinct and pleasurable advantage to make the long winter evenings supplement the long summer days by devoting a portion of them to the seed catalogues and other garden literature.

The selection of varieties of vegetables to grow should be largely influenced by those which form one's daily fare throughout the season. Vegetables which are seldom purchased—unless it be because of their high price or scarcity—may not profitably be cultivated in the home garden. But in the case of high-priced products, then the home garden demonstrates its economic value as enabling one to indulge in otherwise unattainable luxuries. Plainly,

THE VEGETABLE GARDEN

then, one should grow in abundance those things of which most consumption is made. There will be a demand for those vegetables which come earliest in spring—rhubarb, asparagus, radishes, lettuce, and such quick-growing things; and for vegetables which may be stored in the cellar to increase the none-too-generous variety of the winter larder—potatoes, parsnips, carrots, squash, and the like. Sweet corn, beans, peas, and beets, especially those for early greens, cabbage, cauliflower, and tomatoes, will be indispensable summer products which must be provided for.

A little study of the catalogues or of the instructions under the heading of various vegetables elsewhere in this book will show the height of these, the period at which they are in season, and the distance apart they should be planted, and this data will furnish the necessary information as to quantity of seed or number of plants required for a given area.

If the land devoted to the kitchen garden is comprised in the boundaries of a city lot the arrangement will, necessarily, be somewhat different than that which would prevail in the country, where the garden occupies more ground and is more or less retired from observation.

PLANNING THE GARDEN

HOW TO REALLY START THE GARDEN

First of all, draw a plan (to a scale) of the ground at your disposal. Make allowances for paths, borders, etc. It's fascinatingly interesting after you get started. Next, take inventory of your likes and dislikes in vegetables. Put down on paper every vegetable you wish to grow. Then go back to your plan and mark out a definite space or number of rows for the different vegetables. Select early, midseason and late sorts of these vegetables which you like best. This will give you a constant supply of them. When garden operations start, be sure to follow your plan. A disregard of your carefully planned programme may easily spoil results. I can not lay too much emphasis upon this point, since most gardens fail to yield satisfactory crops for lack of adherence to the original plan.

Study the peculiar characteristics of certain vegetables and utilize them to best advantage. Some vegetables thrive even in partially shaded positions, while others require lots of sunshine for best results. Some of the finest lettuce I ever saw was grown between rows of early peas. The two foot tall pea vines, rows running east and west,

THE VEGETABLE GARDEN

would shelter Wayahead, Black Seeded Simpson, etc., which form perfect heads.

Though the pea rows were standing only 2½ feet apart, the lettuce did splendidly since peas root deeply while lettuce is a shallow rooting plant. Keeping the lettuce row free from weeds gives additional cultivation to the pea vines, which will, under such conditions, stand considerable dry weather and still bear heavy crops.

A good many vegetables are of exceedingly slow growth during the seedling stage of development. Take advantage of this by utilizing space between such rows for quick-growing crops. For example, sow beet seed by middle of April and set young lettuce plants between the rows. By the time the beet tops develop, the lettuce will be used.

A distance of 20 inches between the rows is ample for most vegetables in a carefully managed home garden. Tall peas, tomatoes and corn should be allowed at least 2 to 2½ feet and should be staked for best results. The proper thinning out of all kinds of vegetables is advisable. Do not permit root crops to crowd each other in the row. Thin out radishes, beets, onions, turnips, etc., to stand about from 2 to 4 inches apart in the row, accord-

PLANNING THE GARDEN

ing to variety. Beans will yield more and better pods if plants stand 4 to 6 inches apart in the row.

Where space is rather limited, the French method of intensive cultivation may be employed. Here is how it is practiced:—

Combine a packet of spinach seed and carrot seed, mixing seeds thoroughly. Make your row uniformly half an inch deep and sow this mixture in the row. Cover, and soon the quick-growing spinach seed will break the crust, making it easier for the weak carrot seedlings to see the light of day. In four weeks, the spinach may be "thinned" to make room for the slowly developing carrots. In six weeks the spinach will be all used up, and the carrots will find room to develop. If an early carrot, such as Early Scarlet Horn, is selected, this will be ready for the table use by July 15th, when the last may be pulled to make room for endive, celery, late cabbage or any other fall crop.

This method may be employed with quite a number of vegetables. Care should be taken in experimenting along these lines, that kinds are combined having seed of about the same coarseness, but possessing different characteristics as to growth. Lettuce and radishes go well together, so do radishes and parsley, the last named being an exceedingly slow grower. The French gardeners plant extra early radishes, midseason lettuce and turnips in the same row, at one operation. This gives about as ideal a succession as can be worked out.

As to the actual location of the different rows and crops, here is a good rule to follow:—

If the land runs east and west the taller plantings should be on the north, so that the light will not be shut off from the lower growing vegetables. Corn grows so much taller than anything else cultivated that it should, if possible, be placed in the rear. In front of it the few hills of early potatoes which it is possible to grow on a city lot may be planted, as they are the least ornamental of vegetables.

Cabbage and cauliflowers grow of corresponding height, and may be planted side by side and given the same treatment. Tomatoes may follow the potatoes, and so on in the order of height until the front of the garden is reached, and such ornamental vegetables as remain may be placed.

The accompanying diagram will be of assistance, and is quite possible for an ordinary lot of twelve rods by four, allowing eight rods of the rear of the lot for the growing of vegetables.

B	Corn, 18 hills	Corn, 18 hills	L
	"	"	
	1 pint seed	1 pint seed	100
B	Potatoes, 28 hills	Potatoes, 28 hills	L
	1 peck seed	1 peck seed	112
B	Cabbage, 18 plants	Cauliflower, 18 plants	L
	"	"	
	"	"	54
B	Tomatoes, 18 plants	Tomatoes, 18 plants	L
Cucumbers	"	"	Melons
	"	"	108
S	Peppers, 18 plants	Peppers, 18 plants	72 R
	"	"	
S	Egg Plants, 18 plants	Egg Plants, 18 plants	72 R
	"	"	
	Carrots	Carrots	
	Carrots, 1 oz. seed	Carrots, 1 oz. seed	
S	Salsify, 1 oz. seed	Salsify, 1 oz. seed	R
	Parsnips, 1 oz. seed	Parsnips, 1 oz. seed	
S	Parsley	Parsley	R

L—Lettuce   R—Radishes
B—Beets   S—Salsify

This leaves room for several rows of fruit and a generous asparagus bed in the rear.

Liquid manure is one of the best acting fertilizers

CHAPTER FIVE
HOW TO MAINTAIN FERTILITY

THE soil is a working laboratory in which chemical reactions are constantly going on, making the various elements available as plant food. In order that a piece of land shall produce a profitable crop, as much depends upon the mechanical condition of the soil as upon the various chemical elements that it contains which go to make up the structure of the plants grown upon it. Soil is made up of disintegrated rock and decayed vegetable matter, but if it were rock alone it could not support plant life, at least the highly organised plant life upon which we depend for food. In order to support plant life it must have humus, decayed vegetable, and animal matter. Virgin soil contains enough humus to make possible all the necessary chemical changes to produce sufficient plant food, but unless the soil is carefully cultivated and attention paid to the replenishing of it the supply of humus is in great danger of becoming exhausted, and the soil is then said to be "worn out."

Humus is the black or brown material which gives the dark colour to the top ten or twelve inches of soil. Added to the soil, humus increases its water-holding capacity, thereby insuring a more constant soil moisture. It aids in the decomposition of the mineral matter by harbouring bacteria which convert unavailable forms into a condition in which it can be assimilated by plants. It fixes the ammonia, which contains nitrogen, in the soil, so that it is not leached out by rains, and it improves the mechanical condition of the soil by keeping it loose and free, permitting aëration.

The natural supply of humus comes from the decaying leaves and wood of the forest, but as soon as the forests are removed and the land cultivated this supply is cut off. It can be renewed, however, by giving the land periodical dressings of stable manure, green manure, or peat or swamp-muck. These last two are not always available, and when they are, it is doubtful if they can be economically applied to land on account of the cost of hauling and spreading.

Stable manure is undoubtedly the best form in

HOW TO MAINTAIN FERTILITY

which to supply humus, because the soil is receiving at the same time nitrogen, phosphoric acid, and potash, the three most important elements in plant foods. It is vegetable matter that has been partly digested by animals and is in a condition to be more quickly assimilated by plants than is a green manure.

Green manure is supplied by growing a crop of clover, or other leguminous plants, or rye, and turning it under. I have seen comparatively unproductive sandy soils from which nitrogen was leached out by rains as fast as it could be supplied, brought into good tilth and produce large crops by its use. In the small garden, where one cannot afford to lose the time necessary to do this, as it is done in large farming operations, rye or clover can be sown in the fall as soon as the vegetable crops have been removed, or between the rows at the last cultivation of such crops as corn, and whatever growth has been turned under at the time of spring ploughing. I have seen this done with good results on small areas.

The clovers and other leguminous crops are the best green manures because of their ability to absorb and fix free atmospheric nitrogen. If you were to dig up carefully a clover plant and wash away the soil you would find many little nodules on the roots. These little bunches contain bacteria, and it is these little bacteria which collect and convert the free atmospheric nitrogen into an available form for plants to use. Long before the value of these little nodules was recognised it was a known fact that good crops of beans could be produced on land that could not grow a profitable crop of anything else. These bacteria made it possible. In the North the common red clover and rye are the best crops to grow for green manure. The rye is not a legume and cannot fix atmospheric nitrogen, but it makes a heavy growth of foliage, producing when turned under a good amount of humus. From New Jersey south to Georgia the crimson clover will make a good stand and survive the winter. It can be sown any time from July to September; the earlier date is for the northern portion of this territory. The vetches and cow peas have also proven to be valuable green manures.

With the exception of corn and potatoes, crops do not usually do well on land which has just had a green crop turned under, because of the acidity produced by the fermentation. Let the land lay

HOW TO MAINTAIN FERTILITY

for about six weeks before planting and frequently harrow it to compact the soil.

There are fourteen different chemical elements that are necessary for plant growth—namely, carbon, hydrogen, oxygen, nitrogen, phosphorus, sulphur, chlorine, silicon, calcium, iron, potassium, sodium, magnesium, and manganese. The first four are derived either directly or indirectly from the air, the remaining ten are derived from the soil. Virgin soil contains all these soil-derived elements in available forms and in sufficient quantities for plant growth, and it has the ability to absorb the air-derived elements, but our methods of agriculture rob the soil of some of its elements faster than it can convert them into available form for the plants. Therefore we must supply these elements in order to produce good crops.

The best way of renewing these necessary elements is by dressings of stable manure—the droppings from horses, cows, and other domestic animals. Soil enriched by barn-yard manure will yield better crops than soil which has been given chemical fertilisers containing an equal amount of plant food. Whether the manure shall be fresh or well rotted depends upon the conditions. The fertilising constituents of well-decayed manure are more quickly available to the plants than are those in fresh manure, but, on the other hand, fresh manure soon rots and the fermentation of decay assists in rendering soluble hitherto insoluble fertilising constituents of the soil. If the chief object of applying the manure is to improve the mechanical condition of the soil, the greatest benefit will be had by giving fresh manure to heavy clay loams and well-decayed manure to light, sandy loams. On the other hand, if quick action is wanted, greater benefit will be received under ordinary conditions from fresh manure on light soil than on heavy clay loam. On heavy soil decomposition takes place slowly, so it is some time before the plant food becomes available. Often there is no immediate effect the first year. In light soil, unless the season is very dry, the fertilising constituents of fresh manure become available about as fast as the plant is in need of them. There is danger of leaching away of the nitrogen before it can be used by the plants if well-decayed manure is applied to sandy loams. On clay loams there is no danger of this, because of their ability to absorb and retain large quantities of plant food.

HOW TO MAINTAIN FERTILITY

The amount to apply varies with the crop grown, but for ordinary garden crops as much as twenty tons per acre, or about one two-horse load to a 25 × 100-foot plot, can be used; one-half to two-thirds of this amount will give fair results, however, and larger amounts are often used by " truck " growers. This must be thoroughly mixed with the soil by ploughing under and harrowing before the crop is planted.

It is often the case that the soil does not need a complete fertiliser, for only one of the three important plant foods—nitrogen, phosphoric acid and potash—is lacking. If such is the case, it can be easily supplied by one of the various chemical fertilisers on the market.

Before applying these highly concentrated chemical fertilisers I would strongly advise your testing the soil to find out just what is needed. To do it divide the garden into strips, say ten feet wide, and on every other strip apply these special fertilisers, one to a strip, in various quantities and watch the results. One test will probably be sufficient to give the information desired.

Nitrogen is the most expensive of the three essential elements required by plants. It can be had

THE VEGETABLE GARDEN

in three different forms, organic nitrogen, as ammonia, and in nitrates. The most valuable sources of organic nitrogen are dried blood and tankage, which are by-products of slaughter houses, dried fish, and refuse from fish canneries and oil factories, and cotton-seed meal. These contain in every one hundred pounds of bulk the following amount (approximately) of nitrogen: dried blood, ten to fifteen; tankage, seven to nine; dried fish, seven to eight; cotton-seed meal, six to seven. All these substances decay rapidly upon being put in the soil, but not so quickly but that they can be made use of by the plant as soon as they become available. They are particularly valuable on light soils, from which nitrogen in the form of ammonia or nitrates are rapidly leached, and they have the further advantage of making available during the process of fermentation insoluble forms of phosphoric acid and potash. They also furnish small quantities of phosphoric acid. Cotton seed or cotton-seed meal is not used in the North to any extent as a fertiliser, but in the South it is a cheap form of nitrogen. It can be applied alone or in combination with chemical fertilisers. It contains about seven per cent of nitrogen and three per cent of phosphoric acid

HOW TO MAINTAIN FERTILITY

and two per cent of potash. About sixty bushels per acre of the green seed or its equivalent of meal, together with about one thousand pounds of a complete fertiliser, will be a good dressing for the garden.

Nitrogen in the form of ammonia is derived almost exclusively from sulphate of ammonia, the commercial product containing about twenty per cent. This form of nitrogen is easily converted in the soil to nitrate, the form in which it is used by plants, but before being converted it will readily combine with the soil becoming fixed, so that there is no danger of its leaching. This quality makes it very valuable for light, sandy loams and for use in wet seasons, when nitrate of soda would leach from the soil rapidly.

The commonest form of commercial nitrogen is nitrate of soda, which contains about 15.5 per cent of nitrogen. Nitrate of soda dissolves at once upon being put in the soil; it has a strong affinity for water. In this form the nitrogen is at once available to the plants. As it is so soluble, there is danger of its being leached from the soils, especially sandy soils, if more is given than the plants can use in a short time.

Phosphorus is used by plants in the form of phosphoric acid, and there are several forms in which it can be had. The organic forms of nitrogen, which I have mentioned, contain a little phosphoric acid. The most common and most highly concentrated form of phosphoric acid on the market now is superphosphates, or soluble phosphates. These are derived from the phosphate rock secured in South Carolina, Florida, and Tennessee. They are seldom used in their natural state, because but little of the phosphoric acid in them is available as plant food. It is made available by grinding and treating with sulphuric acid. These treated phosphate rocks contain twenty-five to thirty per cent of available phosphoric acid.

Thomas slag, a by-product in the manufacture of steel, has been used frequently as a source of phosphoric acid, but as the supply is limited it cannot always be obtained. It contains about nineteen or twenty per cent of available phosphoric acid and six or seven per cent which is insoluble in soil water.

Bone contains a great deal of phosphoric acid—about twenty-two per cent—and it also contains about four per cent of nitrogen. Bone can be secured in several different forms, such as raw, boiled or steamed, and fine bone. Upon its condition when applied to the land will depend the rapidity with which it will become available to the plants. All the phosphoric acid in raw, broken bone will not become available and used up by the plants in less than four years, because the fat retards decay. For this reason the bone is steamed and ground, and in this condition all the phosphoric acid will have become available in about two years. In steamed bone there is less nitrogen, however, because some of the organic material containing it is removed by the process.

Other forms of bone which are sometimes used as fertilisers are bone-black and bone-ash. They are much less valuable, because in their preparation by burning all the organic matter is driven off, therefore they contain no nitrogen, and it lessens the amount of phosphoric acid somewhat.

Tankage is the only other material containing phosphoric acid which is sufficiently common in the trade to warrant consideration. The fertilising content of tankage varies according to what it is made from; the higher its percentage of phosphoric acid the less nitrogen it contains and *vice versa.* At present there are five different grades on the market containing anywhere from seven to nineteen or twenty per cent of phosphoric acid. Its price also varies according to its contents.

When soluble phosphoric acid is added to the soil it becomes " fixed " or insoluble by combining with lime, making lime phosphate, or by uniting with iron or aluminum. The former is the most desirable form, as the phosphoric acid in lime phosphate is more readily reconverted into available forms for plant use by the fermentation of organic material in the soil than are the phosphates of iron and aluminum. Therefore, to insure the formation of lime phosphate, it is necessary that the soil should be well supplied with lime and humus.

The other element, potash, which it is necessary to add to the soil is derived mainly from muriate or chloride of potash, sulphate of potash, and unleached hardwood ashes. Most of the potash, other than the ashes, comes from mines in Germany. Sulphate of potash is a much better form to use because the chlorides in muriate of potash seem to have an unfavourable effect on crops. This is particularly true of tobacco and potatoes. Kainit is frequently offered and sold by dealers.

HOW TO MAINTAIN FERTILITY

Its potash is in the form of sulphates, but as it contains large quantities of chlorides mixed with it, it has the same general effect on plants as muriate of potash.

High-grade sulphate of potash contains forty-eight to fifty-one per cent of potash, low grade twenty-eight to thirty per cent, kainit twelve to fourteen per cent, muriate of potash (eighty to eighty-five per cent pure), fifty to fifty-three per cent, and unleached wood ashes four to eight per cent. Never use leached-wood ashes as a direct fertiliser, as they usually contain but a small percentage of potash.

When muriate of potash is used the chlorides combine with the lime, forming chloride of lime, which is very soluble and leaches away rapidly, a distinct disadvantage, and it makes applications of lime necessary. Further, the presence of large quantities of chloride of lime in soil is apt to be detrimental to plants.

Greater effect is had from the use of these potash fertilisers on light, sandy soils, humus soils, or those containing lime, than on heavy clay loams. On the light soils, to get the full value of the potash applied, there should be in it considerable

THE VEGETABLE GARDEN

lime. Without the lime the soluble potash leaches out rapidly.

I have described these different fertilising elements at some length in order that if the reader desires to mix his own fertilisers he will know what each contains. Unless one uses only a small quantity of these commercial fertilisers it is a distinct advantage in point of cost to do the mixing at home rather than to buy the ready-mixed materials. Not only is it necessary to pay the manufacturer for mixing them, but you also pay freight on earth, which is always added to these ready-made fertilisers as fillers. Another distinct advantage of home-mixed fertilisers is that the ingredients can be varied according to the needs of plants grown and the condition of the soil.

For an average soil, on which the ordinary garden crops—beets, cabbage, cucumbers, celery, tomatoes, etc.—are being grown, a fertiliser compounded as follows will give good results:

Nitrate of soda............	50 pounds
Sulphate of ammonia......	100 pounds
Dried blood..............	150 pounds
Acid phosphate...........	550 pounds
Muriate of potash.........	150 pounds

HOW TO MAINTAIN FERTILITY

An equal amount of sulphate of potash can be supplemented for the muriate of potash if that form is best for the crop.

This is enough for the spring application to one acre, but it should be supplemented by two or three dressings of nitrate of soda at intervals during the season, giving about one hundred to two hundred pounds each time.

The formula just given reduced to amounts for a small area, say a 25 × 100-foot plot, would be

Nitrate of soda	2½ pounds
Sulphate of ammonia	5 pounds
Dried blood	7½ pounds
Acid phosphate	27½ pounds
Muriate of potash	7½ pounds

and the subsequent dressings of nitrate of soda would be five to ten pounds each.

The ingredients of this formula may be changed; for instance, if bone meal is more accessible, an equal amount can be substituted for the acid phosphate, but the phosphoric acid will not be so quickly available.

When mixing fertilisers great care must be taken to evenly distribute all the ingredients through the mixture. This is best done by putting them in a pile in layers and then throwing them into another pile. Always shovel from the bottom of the pile, throwing the material on the top of the second pile. Three or four turnings will be necessary to thoroughly incorporate all the ingredients.

All these substances which I have mentioned are direct fertilisers, but there are soils from which the full value of these cannot be had without the use of a stimulant or indirect fertiliser. Lime and land plaster or gypsum are used for this purpose.

The reasons for liming the land are: First, that sour or acid soils must be neutralised or made slightly alkaline, because the bacteria which convert the organic forms of nitrogen into the forms of nitrates cannot thrive in acid soils. Second, used in small quantities, it will bind loose, sandy soils. Third, it will flocculate stiff clayey soils, making the passage of water through them easier, lessening the tendency to wash, and permitting better aëration. Fourth, in holding the potash compounds, as already described, and overcoming the bad effect of potash salts containing chlorides.

There are other lesser reasons which it is not

Deep digging, frequent manuring and an occasional application of lime are essential to maintain a high degree of fertility

Cultivation is fertilization in that air and oxygen are just as essential to good crops as potash, phosphates etc.

necessary to discuss here. Gypsum is just as good as lime for all these reasons excepting the correction of soil acidity.

To determine if the soil is sour, one of two methods can be used.

Take a fair sample of the soil and mix enough water with it to make the mass the consistency of thin mortar, then embed in it a strip of blue litmus paper. Allow it to stand half an hour or more, and then, if the paper has turned pink, you will know that the soil is in need of lime.

Another way is to place a tablespoonful of soil in a glassful of water and a teaspoonful of weak ammonia. If, after standing several hours, the liquid becomes dark-brown or black, it is an indication of soil acidity.

The amount of lime necessary will vary according to the soil. Light, sandy loams will not need more than 500 pounds per acre, twenty-five pounds for a plot 25 × 100 feet, but when applied to heavy clay loams, as much as 5,000 or 6,000 pounds can be used, 250 to 300 pounds on a 25 × 100-foot plot. These applications of lime do not need to be made oftener than once in five to seven years.

THE VEGETABLE GARDEN

For heavy, mucky soils, like freshly drained marshes, fresh-burnt lime may be used to good advantage, but in most cases slacked lime, which has been exposed to the weather for some time, is better. A common way in some parts of the country is to bury the lime in soil in the fall and distribute it the following spring. The lime must be evenly distributed and then harrowed in. This should take place several weeks before planting the crop, for if done immediately before seeding, the seeds are very apt to be injured.

Wood ashes contain about thirty-four per cent of lime. These can be used to good effect on sandy or acid soils.

CHAPTER SIX

ON THE SOWING OF SEED

There is no part of the garden work which calls for such nice judgment and careful attention as the sowing of seed. Most of the failures originate right here, and a large share of the blame devoted to the seeds and seedsman, if traced back to its original source, would be found to rest on the ignorance or carelessness of the gardener. In the first place, there is a tendency among a large class of people to get something for nothing or at least at a bargain. This results in the purchase of cheap seeds or premium seeds, or seeds are purchased of the local grocer or seedsman and may, probably, have lain on his shelves from the season before or an even earlier date.

Now, to have a successful garden one must start right by buying good seeds of reliable seedsmen and seeds of plants suited to one's own locality. If, in addition, the seeds have been grown in practically the same latitude, so much the better; it insures a hardy constitution, acclimated to the conditions which prevail in your particular locality. Now, as a general thing, good seed means high-priced seeds or seeds for which one pays a reasonable amount. This is at it should be. One should not expect to raise premium vegetables from cheap, scrub seed, and there is as great a difference in the pedigree of seed as in that of animals.

Then one should not only see that they are securing the best seed that the market affords but they should secure it in time, not wait until they are ready to plant and then rush off an order, hurriedly prepared and half the things needed forgotten and most of the others wrong, and expect to receive them by return mail. The spring of the year is a busy time with the seedsman, and it is but fair to him, as well as just to yourself, to give him a reasonable time to fill your order by getting it in early. If Mr. Jones has ordered an ounce of silver-skin peppers and ruby-king parsnips, there ought to be time allowed for the seedsman to inquire what Mr. Jones really wants, and not be obliged to fill his order by guesswork. Of course he will readily understand that what is wanted is ruby-king peppers and silver-skin onions, but how about the parsnips?

Late in winter or early in spring one should go over their seeds which have been saved from the home garden and ascertain how far they meet the requirements of the coming year. Then a list of such seeds as are not on hand should be made and the catalogues consulted for prices and varieties. The list made up then may, probably will, need frequent revising, and by the time it is mailed to the seedsman may be trusted to supply just about the varieties and quantities wanted. And, speaking of quantity, it will be about as cheap, in a good many cases, to buy by the ounce as by the packet; especially is this the case with those seeds of which it may be necessary to make repeated sowings—as cucumbers, squashes, melons, beans, and the like. A cold, wet spring often entails much replanting, and sufficient seed should be on hand to enable one to replant at once when it is discovered that the first planting is for any reason abortive. Owing to the proneness of seeds of vine plants to rot in the ground if too wet or cold, a much greater quantity of seed is required. Generous planting of these seeds is also necessary on account of the ravages of the squash bug, which must be liberally fed to induce him to leave a plant or two for the garden.

Next in importance to the quality of the seeds is the time in which they are sown. There are a few seeds which may be gotten into the ground as early as it can be worked. Beets, cabbage, lettuce, onions, peas, salsify, spinach, and turnips are all planted for early crops as soon as the ground can be worked, but such early planting of corn, tomatoes, melons, cucumbers, and other heat-loving plants would simply result in the loss of both time and seed.

The condition of the soil, also, has a marked influence on the germination of the seed. When the ground is still wet from the frost in spring it is not in condition for successful sowing of seed; it is better to wait until it has dried sufficiently to be mellow and tractable before sowing any kind of seed. Too dry a soil is seldom a cause of complaint. The thorough firming of the soil over the seed is of the utmost importance—this and the depth at which the seeds are planted—for in sowing seed in the open ground much greater depth is necessary than would be given the same seed in the hotbed.

ON THE SOWING OF SEED

In my early gardening experience I was very ambitious about getting things started at the earliest possible moment and to have things a little in advance of my neighbours, but several years of covering plants in the open ground to protect them from frost has quite cured me of any undue ambition; I am quite willing that my neighbour's tomatoes shall ripen a day or two ahead of mine if in return they will collect blankets, quilts, canvas, and other protective material and spend frosty hours spreading them over tender plants scattered over an acre or two of ground and trail around in the dew of the morning removing them, while I toast my toes by the fire and read my evening paper.

Unless the time and the condition of the ground is entirely favourable, it will be well to plant only a portion of the seed at a time, reserving enough for a second planting should the first fail to come up or the young plants be destroyed in any way.

CHAPTER SEVEN
TRANSPLANTING

It is a question whether the time at which tender plants shall go into the ground is a matter of prudence or of courage. If one has a good hotbed well stocked with plants on which to draw, then " he either fears his fate too much or his deserts are small. Who fears to put it to the touch, and win or lose it all," if the weather and soil are in a favourable condition for planting, for there is no question that one often gains two or three weeks by early planting. Nevertheless, the chances are against it, and it is not to be recommended where plants must be purchased, or all one's stock is put into the ground at once.

It may be accepted as a rule that warm weather early in March or April will be followed by a cold spell in early May, and that plants put into the ground ahead of this period will be apt to suffer, if, indeed, they do not perish outright.

TRANSPLANTING

The kind and condition of the plants will have much importance in deciding the time at which they may be transferred to the open ground. If cabbage plants have been properly hardened off they may go into the ground much earlier than if very tender. For this reason plants which were started from seed sown in September of the previous year and carried through the winter in coldframes or those from seed in spring and well hardened can go into the ground as early as it can be worked in the spring, but tender plants from hotbeds, started the middle of March or first of April at the North, should not be set out before the first of May, and even then should have been well hardened off by exposure to the weather—nights as well as during the day—for a week or more. Cabbage plants which show a whitish-green shade are too tender for outdoor life, and it will be better to wait until they show a film of blue over the foliage. Tender plants, like peppers and egg-plants, should not go into the ground until settled warm weather, which at the North will be any time from the twentieth of May to the first of June.

Before commencing the transplanting of any vegetables the ground should be thoroughly prepared by ploughing and dragging—both ways—and floating off, or if spading is necessary, it should be very thoroughly done, so that the soil is entirely broken up and pulverised, and the steel rake should be used to get the surface into as fine a condition as possible. The lines for the plants should be set and the distance apart the plants are to stand in the rows indicated. Market gardeners use a marker consisting of a long pole with a cross-piece at one end of the length of the distance apart of the rows and provided with a triangular piece of wood, as a marker or peg, at each end. This is drawn over the ground in each direction and a plant set at each intersection of the lines. It is very little more trouble to use a garden line and reel, and the result is much straighter lines. A garden tape, which has the feet marked in red numbers, is handy in this connection, and as a hundred-foot line is inexpensive, it will be found a very profitable thing to have about the garden.

It will much simplify the planting to have the rows marked out and the holes dug before any plants are lifted from the beds. The hotbeds should have been well watered the night before, and if the number of plants is not large, planting may be

TRANSPLANTING

delayed until the late afternoon of the following day. Planting large numbers of plants in this way may be done in several days. Great care should be exercised in lifting the plants from the beds; they should not be grasped by the handful in the hand and pulled up like so many weeds—a process which leaves most of the roots in the ground—but should have the trowel passed well down below their roots and a section lifted carefully out, the plants being separated as they are set. The advantage of this method will be apparent if one will compare the roots of the carefully lifted plants with those pulled up in the usual haphazard way. The latter will have one long root, with a few fragments of side root adhering, while the carefully lifted and separated plant will show a fine mass of fibrous roots, which will at once take hold upon the soil in the new position and begin to feed the plant and produce growth, while the badly lifted plant must first replace the roots of which it was so ruthlessly bereft before it can give any nourishment or assistance to the top.

Only as many plants should be lifted at once as may be gotten into the ground before they wilt. Keeping the plants in good condition until they are safely in the ground is half the battle in transplanting.

In setting the plants, the directions for the several kinds of vegetables as to distance apart of the rows and space between the plants in the row should be followed, but the same general principles must be followed in the transplanting.

A hole should be made for each plant, large enough and of sufficient depth to hold the roots in the same position they occupied in the hotbed and the roots placed so that the plant sets slightly lower than it did in the hotbed. Draw a portion of the soil about the roots and press it down firmly with the hands. If the soil is very dry, fill the hole with water, and when it has nearly soaked away draw up the remainder of the earth and settle this snugly, but not hard, about the plant; after all is done, go over the ground lightly with the trowel, so as to leave a fine dust mulch about the plant.

The work of planting will be much simplified where the plants are set in long rows by setting all the plants in the holes before applying the water; one can then go along the rows with a pail and dipper and fill the holes with water, and by the time the end of the row is reached, the first

TRANSPLANTING

holes will be ready for filling, and by the time all are filled, any moisture which may work to the surface will have had time to appear and may be covered with a dust mulch. The planting should all be looked over carefully before leaving to see if any wet spots appear; when such is the case, they must be immediately covered with fresh, dry earth. No covering or protection of any kind need be given, except in case of frost. The dust mulch takes the place of shingles, paper, or anything used to protect from the sun. Properly planted, with the soil firmly pressed about the roots and well watered and the protecting dust mulch preventing the heating of the soil or evaporation of moisture, the tops exposed to the fresh air and sunshine, the plant is in the best possible condition to withstand the change of position; also, if it has been watered the night before and lifted in the morning before the sun has materially reduced its strength, the plant cells are full of water and will not need to call on the roots for a supply until a time they are in a position to respond.

There is no one fallacy I find so much trouble in overcoming in people I employ about my garden, or with whom I come in contact in gardening matters, as that of the necessity of protecting newly set plants. I was brought up in the orthodox dogmas of gardening and taught to protect everything that went into the ground until it had taken root, and I remember the wearisome hours spent in placing shingles, paper caps, and the like between the plant and any possible rays of the sun; and I especially recall several hundred small plants which were once covered with the most "scientific" of paper caps, provided with an attached stick to thrust into the ground to hold them in place. I spent the leisure hours of several evenings fashioning these out of stiff paper, and I viewed with pride the little army of tents in orderly array that gleamed white in the morning sun. But my pride turned to humiliated dismay when the tents were lifted at eventide that the plants might have the benefit of the night air; fully fifty per cent of my plants lay wilted and dying. The water in the soil, unhindered by any protecting dust mulch, had, under the ardent rays of the sun, drawn to the surface and, confined within the narrow confines of the tents, was rapidly reduced to steam, and the poor plants, confined within a Turkish bath, were literally cooked to death. That ended

TRANSPLANTING

my use of any kind of protection, and I have frequently, in the years that have intervened between that disastrous experience and to-day, set out plants of balsam a foot in height in the hottest sunshine without a sign of wilting—and few plants wilt more readily than these.

Having gotten the plants safely and rightly into the ground, let them alone. This is another much-mooted point. Almost everyone who sets out plants during the day is possessed to go puttering around at nightfall with a watering pot or pail and dipper with which to water the newly set plants. This is not only unnecessary but actually harmful if the plants have been properly set. It destroys the dust mulch and defeats the purpose of all the care in planting. Instead, then, of watering the plants, go over the rows late at night or early in the morning and restore the dust mulch to any part that shows wet.

Should rain occur in a day or two after planting, the ground must be gone over, as soon as it can be worked, with trowel, rake, or hoe, to create a fresh mulch of dust.

There is a prevalent prejudice in favour of planting just before a rain. That is, in certain conditions of the weather, a very good plan to follow. If the rain promises to be a long one, or what is known as a spell of wet weather, the plants may safely go into the ground, but if nothing more than a summer shower threatens, which is likely to be followed by bright sunshine, it will be well to wait until it clears. Bright, settled weather offers the best of conditions for planting, as then one can control conditions. A succession of showers, with bright sunshine, or hot, muggy weather, is the most unfavourable condition; the wet earth, under the influence of a hot sun, steams and cooks, and as there is no fresh wind to carry away the unwholesome vapours, the tender plants suffer as much as we do. Cloudy weather, on the contrary, following after a good rain, affords the very best condition for the establishing of the plant in the ground. As a usual thing the plants will not require watering for several days, but should any appear to suffer, a hole may be made by the side of the plant with trowel or dipper and this filled with water and the dry mulch restored.

In setting some plants in the soil, if of weak growth, it will be well to remove a portion of the top. This is universally done by Dutch gardeners,

Paper collar to protect plant from cut worms   A home-made dibble

Above:—A good type of seed flat in which a small number of seedlings are readily raised

Keep records of all work done, in both book and in form of garden labels carrying variety names and planting dates. Left:—A fine example of intensive cultivation, showing young lettuce between tomatoes

TRANSPLANTING

who remove all but the top leaves of cabbage and cauliflowers, and these two they denude of the upper half of the leaves, and I have found it an advantage in my own practice. It not only relieves the roots of the care of the top to a great extent, but, by lightening the tops, the weight is removed from the stem, which is enabled to retain an upright position. Strip every other plant of its leaves and it will be standing upright when the full-leaved plants are bending weakly under the weight of their tops.

Tomato plants are often " drawn " from crowding and form what is known as a " knee " by bending downward towards the ground and then assuming an upright position at this point when roots form all along the horizontal part of the stem. In setting the plants in the ground, they may be set deep enough to cover this crooked part with advantage. Where the plants have become very crooked and drawn, it is a good plan to make the hole in the form of a shallow trench and lay the plant therein, leaving only the top exposed, first removing the leaves below this point. The exposed part will assume an upright position as soon as growth begins and make fine, stocky plants.

THE VEGETABLE GARDEN

All newly set plants are at the mercy of cutworms, and the rows must be gone over every morning early to see what, if any, damage has occurred over night. Wherever a plant is found cut off, immediate search must be made for the culprit. A moment's search will generally discover him just below the surface of the soil near the decapitated plant. Any loose dirt or rubbish will serve as a hiding place for him, and this tendency may be taken advantage of to trap him by laying pieces of board or chips on the ground near the plant, under which he may hide. But as he does not hide until he has had his meal, this is much like locking the stable door after the horse is stolen; but then, of course, his capture and execution will prevent his eating other plants.

Where the plantings are small, it pays to surround the plants with collars of stiff paper, three or four inches high. These should be pressed into the ground a half inch, and care should be taken to see that there are no worms inside the collar when it is placed. Old tin cans with the bottoms burned out are also a good protection, but the trouble with these is that they must all be gathered up in the fall and disposed of in some way. An-

TRANSPLANTING

other remedy which leaves no after-work is to poison the worms, and this I have found very successful. Cut clover wet with sweetened water and Paris green is often used, but I prefer a mixture of corn meal and Paris green, made thin enough to run, and poured in a ring around the stem of the plant, a little way from it. The only objection to this is when chickens are about, but as no little chickens are likely to be abroad at this time of the year, and large ones should be in confinement, this is of little moment, and the first cultivation will turn it under the soil.

I usually find it necessary to go over the garden every morning for a week, and each time replace more or less of the plants before I am finally rid of the pests.

Cabbages, cauliflowers, and tomatoes are the plants most affected by the cut-worm, but his depredations do not stop in the vegetable garden, as he is equally destructive to the flower garden; and some vine plants can never be secure without an encircling collar of tin or other substance.

CHAPTER EIGHT
INTENSIVE CULTIVATION AND HOW TO PRACTICE IT

Much can be done with even a small garden if carefully planned and planted properly. Instances where small backyard gardens, size 20x20 up to size 30x50 were coaxed to yield from $50 to $100 worth of vegetables in the course of a season are numerous. Nor did it require extra fine soil and a lot of help, but just plenty of planning and scheming ahead of time.

Every successful example of intensive gardening is due to this system:

I. Each row is made to bear at least 3 crops in the course of a season.

II. Each square foot of space is utilized in the most practical manner.

III. Vegetables are selected that will yield the most for space and time devoted to them.

Of course it is desirable that the soil should be friable and of good fertility. But these factors

INTENSIVE CULTIVATION

are not so essential as a careful planning of the garden and planting of only the best seeds procurable. A good deal of sunshine is necessary, though quite a number of vegetables thrive even in shaded gardens. Cultivation of most thorough nature is essential and will, to a certain extent, offset a deficient moisture supply. With a sunny piece of ground, good seeds, a good set of tools and a desire to help nature do her part, no one need go without plenty of vegetables, if suggestions offered in the following paragraphs are accepted and put to a test.

THREE TO FOUR CROPS FROM ONE ROW IN ONE SEASON

With few exceptions, nearly every class of vegetables contains early and late maturing sorts. Some, like radishes, peas, corn, etc., offer even three distinct classes, in early, midseason and late sorts. A thorough study of these things is necessary to help solve the problem how to properly "rotate" the crops in the vegetable garden.

"Rotation of crops" means sowing something else in a row as soon as the first vegetable which it produces is past its best. To illustrate, let us

THE VEGETABLE GARDEN

suppose that spinach is sown in the garden by April 15th. By June 1st, this will be ready for use, rows may be cleaned up and sown to bush beans. Select an early sort like Bountiful or Sure Crop Wax, which will bear the best part of its crop between the middle and end of July. Then pull up the bushes, and sow winter radishes or turnips, which will be ready to harvest after the first light frosts in October.

Or you may sow early peas in April. In 50 to 60 days from date of planting, Market Surprise, Little Marvel, Gradus, etc., will have borne their crop, when vines should be promptly removed to make room for beets. These beets, if planted the middle of June, will be ready for table use by middle of August, when the rows may be cleared to make room for lettuce which will be in its prime throughout the early fall.

Any number of schedules like these may be planned and worked out successfully by the gardener who is anxious to make the most of his opportunities. Not only will he be benefited by a constant supply of delicious crisp vegetables, but keeping the ground constantly busy will prevent weeds from taking possession.

INTENSIVE CULTIVATION

However, the true test whether such intensive cultivation is worth while depends largely on the relative space available to the gardener. There is no "right" or "wrong" about it; each must judge for himself according to conditions.

CHAPTER NINE
TOOLS WHICH MAKE GARDENING EASY

The number of tools which it is really necessary for one to have is not large; but if the amateur gardener tries to get along with a hoe, a rake, and a spade, he is sure to have long, tedious hours of hard work. "Working" the soil is the very foundation, the beginning of gardening. More than all the fertilizing and all other attention as growth develops will *through tillage* (which is "working"), before the plants are set out or even the seeds are sown, insure the future welfare of the crops. Tillage opens up the deeper parts of the soil below the surface, thus admitting air and permitting drainage of the surplus surface moisture. It opens the depths to chemical oxidization, and, by its mechanical action of abrasion of particle against particle, it makes the constituents of the soil available to the plant as actual food. A garden that is not deeply tilled before it receives the crop can never be brought to proper responsiveness by subsequent

TOOLS WHICH MAKE GARDENING EASY

surface treatment. This is a cardinal principle of garden work, well recognized by the agriculturist but often, far too often, neglected by the occasional or avocational worker. An unworked soil cannot receive and incorporate additional plant food given as fertilizer, and in this one fact alone may be found the answer to many complaints of failure later in the season. Tillage also incorporates with the soil the organic material that is on the surface, whether that be a natural accession or in the form of top-dressings by spreading manure. A tilled soil will get along, too, in a period of drought when a soil neglected in this respect will demand water.

Too much insistence cannot be put on this necessity of tillage. It is the oldest of all the practices of the garden and farm, and its paramount importance is being more fully appreciated, its reasons better and better understood, as the years roll on.

The ancient Assyrians and Egyptians tilled their soil with a pointed stick, and we of to-day have not found anything of more importance, and indeed our modern plow is but a pointed stick very slightly modified so as to turn the soil as well as to break into it.

THE VEGETABLE GARDEN

The plow does easily on a broad scale what the spade does in a restricted area. We have learned however, that in the matter of the soil, as in any other activity, the form of the tool or implement may be modified or adapted to fit the special conditions of the worker. But this is merely adapting the teachings of experience to serve our convenience. Just because the working of the soil is so ancient, so fundamental, and so universal, and because the primitive tool can do the operation successfully, gardeners as a whole have been slow to realize the virtues of special adaptations of modern tools and the possibilities they possess for the efficient worker who wants to make every move count the utmost. Because a spade, a fork, a rake, and a pick will accomplish all that may be necessary, there is a tendency to let well enough alone; but when the intelligent gardener is doing his own work he may well pause to consider whether he is using the most effective tool for accomplishing the desired result. Remember, a good workman uses good tools. The very best cannot be too good, and anything that increases the actual result while diminishing the actual labor is worth while, and justifies attention.

TOOLS WHICH MAKE GARDENING EASY

Now, there are many accessory tools that the gardener should consider, and manufacturers have of late done much in offering improvements for special purposes. The fact is that the tool manufacturer has been ahead of the market for some time. True the gospel of the wheel-hoe has been pretty well accepted by now, but that is to be taken only as one example of the opportunities at hand. It may be a small matter at first glance to see there are differences in trowels, and to many people a trowel is a trowel—just that, and nothing more. Yet a moment's use will convince that the long, narrow Slim Jim type is infinitely better adapted for "thinning-out" in the rows than the board planting trowel that lifts too wide a spread, and where much bulb planting is done an extra broad, extra short tool is a comfort and relief. There are spades and shovels: the one stout, straight, with an even cutting edge, that will penetrate the compacted earth; the other a scoop set at a different angle for lifting; yet how often do we see the beginner equipped with a shovel trying to dig? And dig, in the sense of tillage, he cannot with such a tool. Use a spade for digging, and a shovel for shoveling or scooping.

THE VEGETABLE GARDEN

When so obvious a mistake is made in a tool of elementary type it is no wonder that the proper appreciation of more refined implements is confused. The variety of such that the present day gardener has before him is bewildering to the new comer, yet it may be accepted as a truism that every one has its real use and will do some one job at least particularly well. The big question is what is the job in your garden that irks most and is there a tool to ease it?

Broadly speaking, tools that help may be divided into distinct groups:

1. Tools to till the land.
2. Accessories to actual planting operations.
3. Machines of defense against insects or fungous diseases.

Those that compose the second group enter very little into the work of the home gardener, and may, for this reason, be eliminated from present discussion. Plant-setting machinery, fertilizer sowers, seeding machinery, etc., are implements largely called for by growers interested in quantity production. Their usefulness is limited almost entirely to market gardeners.

The simplest job in the garden—digging—becomes hard work, if you attempt to do it with the wrong tool. Spading with a shovel, or shoveling with a spade, makes the initial effort a hardship.

Heavy soils call for a spade; light soils are better handled with a spading fork made like a skeleton spade with flat tines; then the round tine fork is used for lifting and tossing light material only. Because of the great difference in soils, even on one and the same estate, every initial garden-making equipment should contain both spading fork and spade.

Then there is the pickaxe, the two-pronged form of it called grubbing-hoe, the rake, trowel, garden-line, wooden labels for marking rows, a strong knife, raffia or soft twine, possibly two types of cultivators (the cutting-blade, and the tooth) which make the maximum output of real work. If you ask "Why a pickaxe?" remember that it not only breaks but lifts obstacles and is invaluable in clearing, and in the skilled hands of some classes of emigrant labor it is a veritable "do all" to dig, pulverize, rake, level, make furrows, hill; and is after all merely the primitive pointed stick made into iron and set with a handle.

In choosing a tool, attention should be paid to

the joining of the handle and the metal part. Seventy-five per cent. of any subsequent trouble starts with a poor connection there. A "strap" union is desirable for any tool that is put to any real strain of leverage.

Even in the elemental tools a great variety of shapes is available, especially among hoes, and a few different types will add to one's comfort. A pointed one for close work, and a long handled cultivator combining the pointed hoe with a three- or five-pronged scratch-weeder will fill the initial needs; although a scuffle or Dutch hoe for surface tillage and weed cutting is also a genuine help.

As has been mentioned above, the wheel-hoe is already well known, and its further development into a combination tool of rake, plow, and hoe in the modern wheel-hoe cultivator (of which the two best known for general purposes are the Planet Jr., and Iron Age) was a simple set. Where the garden exceeds one-eighth of an acre in size, and the work of maintenance devolves upon one pair of shoulders, a machine tool of this nature is almost an essential.

In the evolution of the wheel-hoe attention has been paid to the common soil conditions confront-

TOOLS WHICH MAKE GARDENING EASY

ing gardeners in most sections. Thus, the original five-pronged scratch-weeder, designed upon the principle of the human hand, takes on new power through the curved cultivator tooth, which in the Liberty has reached its greatest perfection. The old-fashioned, two-pronged grubbing hoe is present in the powerful plow shears, reversible, to either break the ground or hill the rows, as may be required. Such attachments form part of the outfit of every complete modern wheel-hoe.

The principle of the old Dutch scuffle-hoe reappears in improved form in the rocker-blade of the modern Gilson weeder which utilizes both the forward stroke and the backward pull of the arm that guides it.

Disc cultivators or cutting rollers, which finely pulverize soil inclined to be lumpy, are found in other types of combination tools and are especially adapted for light soils in the Perfection; whereas for heavy soils there are others such as the Barker cultivator, which combines the advantages of digging-teeth, cutting blade, and revolving knives. A recent application of ingenuity in the Triplex does away with all loose parts and extra tools for adjusting the different attachments, and the cutting blade, cultivator teeth, and plowshare are mounted on a single revolving pivoted axle.

Tools for defense against outside attacks of bugs and fungus are in reality a very recent development and have attained almost over night a degree of perfection that seems to leave little to be desired, and they come in various sizes and styles, varying accordingly in price. For the man who takes the raising of the crops just as seriously as the initial effort of making the garden, quite a number of modern appliances are available. The old-fashioned sifters with which we still apply the common remedies against chewing insects, are gradually being supplanted by the more powerful duster guns, and blowing apparatus. Insecticides in dust form will often do more good than liquids and are often easier to apply. The spray pump in its various forms, however, will continue to be the standard appliance with which to keep the garden well. Most of them, from the little hand apparatus to the big horse-drawn, motor-driven power sprayers for extensive orchard work, are now operated by air pressure which forces the liquid in a continuous stream. The perfection of quite a variety of nozzles, too, adds to the pleasure of doing

The modern wheelhoe is now indispensable in even the small garden. The two-wheel type shown here is considered the most practical. Right:—The power tool for the garden has come to stay. About a dozen kinds and models compete for the user's favour

For heavy clay soils, the tooth-type of hand cultivator is best. (Liberty type shown here). Above: The modern adaptation of the old Dutch scufflehoe—The Gilson Weeder which is the tool "par excellence" to kill surface weeds on light soils

TOOLS WHICH MAKE GARDENING EASY

this work right. Perhaps the most popular of the spray pumps to-day are the Knapsack and Auto-spray types.

The fact that more than 90 per cent. of annual plant growth is water should bring home to the gardener the tremendous responsibility of supplying the crops adequately when nature may deny it in many sections, and in certain seasons.

Much progress has been made during the last twenty years in devices for carrying and distributing water in nature's own way. Excepting for special work in the greenhouse, or where gardening is done on a very limited scale, the old-fashioned watering can has gone into the discard. Extensive irrigation systems of various kinds—underground, on the ground level, or overhead—are now possible wherever a normal water pressure is to be had. Many attractive small devices also help to solve this problem for the lawn and border. Water fans not more than two pounds in weight, which throw streams of water from twenty to thirty feet in alternating directions; oscillating sprinklers of other types, to cover a complete circle up to fifty feet in diameter; and many others, may simply be attached to the regulation garden hose, and a turn of the faucet will set the apparatus automatically to work. Water passing a long distance through the air, falling in a simulation of rain, is found to be very beneficial.

In addition to the various accessories already mentioned, a garden line will be found indispensable. Get a good linen line and keep it on a reel. One hundred feet of line and a first-class reel will cost about $1. Keep it dry, or dry it out if it becomes wet, and it will last for years.

CHAPTER TEN
ON THE GROWING OF VARIOUS VEGETABLES

THERE are several forms of vegetables which, while the culture is not specially dissimilar, may yet, for convenience, be divided into five classes: those the edible part of which is produced beneath the surface of the soil and are known as root vegetables; those which set fruit above ground; those whose fruit is produced on vines; such plants as are used entire, as lettuce and the various greens, and those perennial forms which include the asparagus, artichokes, rhubarb and horse-radish, and the like.

We will first consider the general culture of the plants which produce heads, pods, ears, or other fruit, and which may be roughly designated as head or pod vegetables. They are presented in the following pages in order of their relative importance to the home gardener from an economical standpoint.

TOMATOES

Start tomatoes by sowing seed in a hotbed in spring, or start them in flats in the house and plant them in the open ground when all danger of frost is passed. They require well-manured soil, and when there is a limited supply of fertilizer, it will be well to put two or three spadefuls in each hill, spreading it over a couple of square feet of surface, as the tomato makes considerable root growth. Plant in rows, four feet apart each way if no support is to be given, three feet if the plants are to be grown on racks or trellises.

To let a tomato plant spread on the ground and grow as it will is wasteful. During the past ten years perhaps a dozen different methods of growing pruned plants have been tried out. The fruit produced under such natural conditions is inferior in size to that of the pruned plant, is frequently ill-shaped and of uneven ripening; and the fruit that does develop normally is subject to rot and attack by insects. Records over a number of seasons show the average loss of fruits from such causes to be about 25 per cent. of the whole.

The tomato is an exceedingly rank grower, and

THE GROWING OF VARIOUS VEGETABLES

unless its tendency to make a big plant is checked and directed into other channels, it will make about ten times as much herbage as is necessary. Different methods of growth, of course, necessitate different methods of staking.

Under home garden conditions the general practice is to provide a six foot stake for each plant and to reduce that plant early in its life to the three strongest branches. This is all right with most varieties but there are exceptions. For example, Ponderosa, the strongest and rankest growing of any, should not be allowed more than two branches for the simple reason that the plant is not strong enough to support all the fruit that three branches would bear. I have seen heavy clusters of Ponderosa ripped down the stems, because the weight was too great for the branches to support. On the other hand, the smaller fruited varieties (Manyfold, for example) may have four branches trained up the stake.

When it comes to blight resistance here are the best and most distinct types, in order of their relative merit: Globe, purple; Bonny Best, bright red; Manyfold, bright red; John Baer, bright red; Stone, bright red; Coreless, scarlet; Beauty, purple; Magnus, purple; Ponderosa, purple; Earliana, scarlet.

This would seem to indicate that on the whole, the scarlet varieties are more blight-resistant than the purple ones, with the exception of Livingston's Globe which, as a blight resister, is in a class of its own. Globe is really the variety that has made Florida famous as a producer of perfect tomatoes in recent years.

In the fall, at the approach of hard frost, the green tomatoes may be gathered and placed on racks in a warm, sunny position, where they will continue to ripen for some time, or the plants may be dug up, the roots wrapped in burlap, and hung in a warm, sunny place, where the fruit will ripen very well; I have kept them in the barn until November in this way. Or use may be made of an empty hotbed, in which the green tomatoes are placed on racks or on a bed of straw, and so continue to enjoy them far beyond their usual season.

In conclusion I give here the names of ten sorts of tomatoes that have proven their merit conclusively throughout America. One dozen plants each of an early pink and purple sort and two dozen

THE GROWING OF VARIOUS VEGETABLES

plants of two main crop varieties supply all the tomatoes a family of six can eat, with a surplus of 5 bushels for canning—under favourable soil and season conditions.

NAMES OF SORTS	FIRST FRUIT RIPENED AFTER	WEIGHT OF AVERAGE FRUIT IN OUNCES	SEASON OF BEARING	AVERAGE NUMBER FRUITS PER PLANT
Red or Scarlet				
Spark's Earliana	100 days	6	Short, 2 pickings	15
Chalk's Early Jewel	108 days	7	Long, 4 pickings	19
Stone	116 days	9¾	Late, 3 pickings	20
Coreless	120 days	9½	Late, 3 pickings	15
Dwarf Stone	114 days	6¼	Late, 3 pickings	12
Pink or Purple				
June Pink	98 days	6	Short, 2 pickings	15
Beauty	108 days	7	Early, 3 pickings	16
Globe	114 days	7¼	Early, 4 pickings	18
Magnus	116 days	7	3 pickings	20
Trucker's Favorite	116 days	6½	Late, 3 pickings	16

BEANS

Are a tender class of vegetables, and the seed of any varieties should not be planted out until the nights and soil are warm. Usually the middle of May, at the North, will be found to be quite early enough. In cold, wet soil the seed will decay instead of growing, while the opposite is true where the seed is given a warm location and a warm, sandy soil. The soil should be deeply prepared and well enriched with old manure.

THE VEGETABLE GARDEN

The seed of bush varieties should be sown in drills, two feet apart, and the beans dropped two inches apart in the row and covered two inches deep, treading down the earth after planting.

If the beans are to be used for string beans or fresh shell beans, they may be planted every two weeks for a succession, but for dried beans to use with pork in winter, should be planted early and kept well cultivated and clean until the pods ripen in the fall.

Beans should not, for best results, be planted in a low, wet place or in too much shade. They must not be worked or handled when wet, as this will cause them to mildew. Therefore a warm, sunny position, where they will dry quickly in the morning, is best.

One quart of bean seed will plant a hundred feet of drill and give sufficient beans for a good-sized family. They may be planted for a succession of string beans up to the fifteenth of August. Pole varieties yield much larger crops than the bush forms, and by training to strings, wire netting, etc., may be planted close up to the garden-fence or the poultry-yard, or serve as a screen to hide outbuildings or parts of the garden if desired. The expense

THE GROWING OF VARIOUS VEGETABLES

of poles is, however, avoided by planting only the bush varieties.

The varieties most generally cultivated are the following:

VARIETY NAME	READY FOR TABLE IN	LENGTH OF POD (INCHES)	SEASON OF BEARING
Bountiful	60 days	6½	6 weeks
Full Measure	65 days	6	4 weeks
Fordhook Favorite	70 days	5½	5 weeks
Keeney's Stringless Refugee	80 days	5	Until frost
Burpee's New Kidney Wax	60 days	6½	6 weeks
Sure Crop Wax	65 days	6¼	Until frost
Brittle Wax	65 days	5½	6 weeks
Keeney's Stringless Refugee Wax	75 days	5	Until frost

HIGHEST QUALITY LIMA BEANS

In one respect the two great American vegetables, corn and lima beans, are alike—you *must grow them yourself,* gather them when "just right," and prepare promptly, or the elusive "quality" will not be there at mealtime. The rich, marrow-like, peculiarly characteristic flavour of lima beans cannot be canned, captured by drying, or gotten hold of in any other way than via the home garden.

Both the tall or climbing, and dwarf or bush limas are of specific usefulness. The dwarf sorts are unquestionably the earlier, but the very much longer branches of the tall sorts bear more pods, and consequently their yield is greater; and notwithstanding the introduction of very large-podded dwarf sorts, the pole limas generally surpass in size both of pods and shelled beans. Where garden space is limited and poles are not available, pole limas may be grown along fences or trellises, thus serving the treble purpose of creating shade, hiding unsightly objects, and yielding food.

As to difference in flavour between bush and pole limas I can truthfully say there is none. A great deal depends at what stage of development the pods are picked and how soon after picking the beans are shelled and cooked. Thirty minutes of cooking may bring out the flavour to perfection while forty-five minutes may neutralize it.

Still, a great leeway is possible in connection with these various factors if you press into service pedigreed quality kinds of proven behaviour; and it is in the endeavour to introduce you to limas that *always behave,* that I first mention:

Fordhook Bush Lima is the largest podded form of the old-fashioned "fat" or potato lima. The pods average 5 inches long, are borne in pairs or double pairs and contain on an average four large, thick, green-skinned beans that truly have no superior in flavour. (Incidentally, here is a "tip": whenever you see a green-skinned lima, make up your mind that it is far superior in flavour to the white or yellow-skinned bean). A week to ten days after Fordhook has yielded its first picking, the Burpee-Improved brings us its large, flat pods equal in size to any pole variety. The pods average 5½ inches long and contain on an average 5 beans which, in the green stage, are as large as those of the largest pole limas.

The introduction of these two sorts marked the dawn of a new era in bush limas for, popular as old Burpee's Bush Lima, Quarter Century, or Wonder Bush are to-day, both Fordhook and Burpee-Improved are bound to supersede as soon as seeds can be produced in sufficient quantity. The third of the really pedigreed bush limas is Extra Early Wilson or Extra Early Giant Bush, a comparatively new comer which is the product of persistent selection for earliness. Its pods do not average any larger than those of Fordhook, and contain flat beans which bulk less, but they are ready for picking from 5 days to a week before any other bush variety with the exception of the old Wood's Prolific. This however is fairly obsolete.

THE VEGETABLE GARDEN

THE WORTH WHILE TALL OR CLIMBING SORTS

As in the case of bush limas, the pole varieties started to make most rapid strides in popular favour after a new variety some twenty years ago almost revolutionized lima bean growing. Up to 1900, Large White Lima and its improved form, King of the Garden, were the recognized leaders among pole limas. They required such a long season, however, that in most sections growers had to be satisfied with gathering about half the pods set, for the frost would gather the other half. Then came Henderson's Leviathan, marking the first forward step toward shorter seasons of development for pole limas. Its pods are not so large as those of the older kinds, nor are the beans, but within 100 days Leviathan perfects a good portion of the pods that set early, and, where frost stays away for four months, it is a most prodigious yielder of handsome pods, borne in large clusters.

Some years ago a specialist on the Pacific Coast started to experiment in selecting pods bearing a majority of green-tinted beans. And four years

THE GROWING OF VARIOUS VEGETABLES

of constant effort in one direction produced highly gratifying results. In honour of its birthplace, which is the home of all that is good in limas, the new variety was called Carpinteria; and in Carpinteria Lima we have unquestionably the very highest quality pole lima in cultivation to-day. In general character of pods or bearing qualities it does not differ greatly from Leviathan except that the shelled beans are more elongated and that all of them have the desirable green tint. In season of bearing it will prove slightly earlier than Leviathan, yielding the second picking when Leviathan is just perfecting its first pods.

Truly the leader of them all for size, Burpee's Giant Podded is actually what its name implies. Monstrous pods 6 to 8 inches long, containing from 5 to 7 beans an inch or more in diameter, are ready to please those who look for size. And notwithstanding these extraordinary dimensions, the young green beans are quite thin-skinned and tender. Where long growing seasons prevail and size is wanted this Giant Podded form will find a ready welcome.

SWEET CORN

Is one of the more tender vegetables the seed of which should not be planted until all danger of frost is passed. This, at the North, will be as late as the twentieth of May, though a chance crop may be planted by May 1st on light, warm soil. One quart of seed will plant two hundred hills, which should be made three feet apart each way. The seed should be planted in slightly raised hills, dropping a number of kernels in each hill to allow for any failing to sprout; after the corn is up, these extra plants should be pulled out, leaving three plants in a hill. The extra early sorts may be planted in rows two and a half feet apart, and the hills eighteen inches apart. Plant the seed half an inch deep, and either tramp upon it or pat it down firmly with the hoe. Where the ground is not very heavily manured, a tablespoonful of phosphate may be placed in each hill with benefit.

When the corn has attained three or more feet in height, it will be well to go through the rows and pull out all side shoots and those which will not set ear, allowing the entire strength of the plant to go to the making of corn.

THE GROWING OF VARIOUS VEGETABLES

The green shoots removed makes excellent feed for the horse, cow, or pig, and is greatly relished by them. Corn is, of all garden vegetables, the most economical to grow, as there is absolutely no waste, such corn as may not be used for the table making the finest feed for the poultry in winter, especially for the fattening of cockerels, and the cornstalks, if cut before they are too dry, makes excellent fodder for stock of any kind.

Corn may be planted every two weeks, for a succession, until the middle of July.

For early corn, one must plant the extra early varieties, such as the Early Dawn, Golden Bantam, or the Early Catawba, but for toothsome sweetness there is no corn to equal Country Gentleman, and the later the season the sweeter and better it is. We are now—October 7th—eating White Evergreen that is far better and sweeter than the earlier planting of the same variety, though we have had several sharp frosts—frosts that have badly cut the field corn; but the sweet corn, being somewhat protected by trees, has suffered little, if any, injury.

Corn should be cultivated thoroughly and constantly as long as it is safe to work among it; this

THE VEGETABLE GARDEN

will admit of half a dozen cultivations each way at least, and at the end of this time the ground should be in the condition that few, if any, weeds will appear.

Here is a list of varieties that will provide ears of top-notch quality throughout the season. Where space permits, plant the entire assortment for perfect succession. If room for only one sort, "stick" to Golden Bantam.

VARIETY NAME	READY FOR USE	COLOR	LENGTH OF EAR	NUMBER OF ROWS
Early Dawn	75 days	White	6 inches	10 rows
Earliest Catawba	80 days	White	6 inches	10–12 rows
Golden Bantam	80 days	Yellow	6 inches	8 rows
Howling Mob	85 days	White	8 inches	12–14 rows
Crosby's Twelve Rowed	90 days	White	6 inches	12–14 rows
White Evergreen	93 days	White	8 inches	16–18 rows
Seymour's Sweet Orange	93 days	Yellow	8 inches	10–12 rows
Country Gentleman	95 days	White	10 inches	irregular
Golden Rod	95 days	Yellow	8 inches	8 rows
Golden Cream	96 days	Yellow	6 inches	Irregular

CABBAGE

At the North cabbages are usually started in coldframes or hotbeds early in March and planted out as soon as danger of killing frosts is passed. They succeed best in a deep, rich soil, heavily manured, and in some localities cannot be grown successfully on the same ground year after year; in other sections this does not seem to make any

Two never failing quality kinds, Golden Bantam (above) and White Evergreen, the finest type of ever popular Stowell's Evergreen

Well-grown cabbage is quite an ornamental feature of the kitchen garden. Surehead, shown here, is the best all-round strain of Premium Flat Dutch Type

THE GROWING OF VARIOUS VEGETABLES

difference, and in my own garden they have grown in the same spot for several successive seasons.

They should be well cultivated and kept free from weeds. The cabbage worm is very troublesome in some sections, but in the private garden need not make any serious trouble. As soon as the little white butterflies appear, the plants should be watched for the presence of eggs, and when these are found and removed, the worms are disposed of; the eggs will be found in a small yellow patch on the underside of the leaves; they are quite conspicuous, and easily removed.

Early cabbage is sometimes given to cracking as soon as ripe, and must be used at once, as the new growth commences then. To prevent this, the roots may be cut off on one side of the plant as soon as the head has attained its growth and the plant tipped over on its side; this checks growth, and the head will then keep for some time.

For late cabbage, seed is sown in the open ground from April to June, and the plants transplanted into permanent rows early in July, setting the plants in rows two and a half feet apart and two feet apart in the rows, which is the space allowed the early cabbage. The cabbage fly is likely to trou-

THE VEGETABLE GARDEN

ble the young seedling cabbage plants, and they should be dusted with wood ashes, air-slacked lime, tobacco dust, or road dust, as soon as the plants are above ground; this should be done while yet the plants are wet with dew in the morning.

CABBAGES BEST FOR GENERAL USE

A packet of cabbage seed contains more than enough to raise all the plants you and your neighbour can use. For the average home garden, a dozen plants of an early and of a midseason sort and two dozen each of a late and a Savoy cabbage fill all requirements.

VARIETY NAME	NUMBER DAYS FROM SEED TO HEADS	TYPICAL SHAPE	MOST SUITABLE SOIL
Early Jersey Wakefield	100–110	Conical	Medium light for early planting
Eureka First Early	100–110	Round	Medium light for early planting
Allhead Early	120–125	Flatround	Medium light for early planting
Copenhagen Market	100–110	Round	Strong, medium heavy
All Seasons	130–135	Round	Grows well in any good soil
Succession	135–140	Flatround	Medium light to fairly heavy. Not too wet
Premium Flat Dutch	150–160	Flat	Medium light to fairly heavy. Not too wet
Danish Ballhead	150–160	Round	Strong soil, free from stem rot bacteria
Impr. American Savoy	150–160	Round	Average good
Danish Round Red	150–160	Round	Strong, rather heavy

CAULIFLOWERS

Are given practically the same culture as cabbages, starting the plants in the hotbed in April

THE GROWING OF VARIOUS VEGETABLES

and planting out when danger of heavy frost is past.

Particular attention must be paid to the young plants for the first week, as they are very liable to be cut off by cut-worms. When this occurs, the only remedy is to replace the plants with others from the coldframe.

Spring outdoor-started plants will not give very early cauliflowers, but will come on in July and August, and are used for pickling as well as for the table. Where it is desired to grow cauliflowers for the summer use on the table, it will be necessary to start the plants very early in the hotbeds, or in the South start them in the fall and winter in coldframes, and plant out as early in spring as the ground can be worked. The wintering in coldframes hardens them, so that this early planting is possible, which is not the case with the tender greenhouse or hotbed plants. At the North, plants of the cabbage and cauliflower cannot well be kept over in coldframes.

If there is a rather wet, low spot in the garden, it may be used for the cauliflower better than for almost any other vegetable.

The cabbage worm often causes serious trouble

with the cauliflowers, and as soon as the little white butterflies are seen hovering about the plants, search must be made for the eggs and these destroyed. They will be found on the underside of the leaves—a little patch of yellow eggs—and are easily removed.

As soon as the curd, or head, is set and is as large as a teacup, the plant must be tied up by drawing the tips of the leaves together and tying them with a string. This must never be done, however, when it is wet with rain or dew. Mid-day, on a bright day, is the best time for the work. If tied up when the leaves or curd is wet, the heads will decay; if not tied up, a second growth will quickly start and ruin the heads.

Unlike cabbage, cauliflowers cannot be kept during winter, being very perishable, and must be used within a day or two of attaining perfection, or the flavour is impaired. Cauliflower is one of the most delicious of table vegetables and should come into general use; it is far more delicate in flavour than cabbage, and one of the most attractive vegetables which appears on the table.

Very good cauliflower may be raised by the ordinary culture given cabbage—cauliflowers averaging eight or nine inches across—but to grow really fine heads, a foot or fifteen inches in diameter, snowy white, and perfect, requires special culture. To this end the plants must have an abundant water supply during the dry months of the summer, watering every other day, and cultivating between times. Liquid manure should be given at least once a week, and twice a week will be better. With this extra care, cauliflowers may be produced that will be the envy of one's neighbours, and may contend for the blue ribbon at the county fair.

Cauliflowers do better during cool weather, and are at their best in the late days of September and October. A light frost seems to benefit rather than injure them, and tying the leaves over the curd protects them from even a severe frost, but when a frost has cut the leaves badly, the curds should be gathered and used, as decay sets in very soon after.

PEAS

Sow peas as early as the ground can be worked in spring; old gardeners usually claim that they like to have the last snow find their peas in the ground; certain it is that peas like a cool soil, and often fail to germinate when the weather and soil are warm. The dwarf varieties are usually preferred for the private garden, but will not bear as heavily as the taller sorts; but as these require brushing, the difference in labour is by many considered to more than offset their extra productiveness. Poultry netting makes ideal support for the tall-growing sorts, and if rolled up and stood in a dry place after the peas are gathered, will last a lifetime.

The wrinkled varieties are far ahead in tender sweetness of the smooth varieties, but as they are not as hardy, they should be planted in well-drained warm, sandy ground for the first planting.

Peas may be planted for a succession every two weeks up to the middle of June, then should be discontinued until the middle of August, when sowings of the extra-early varieties may be made for a late crop.

In planting, sow in double rows, six to eight inches apart, the rows from two to three feet apart. Plant the seed four inches deep and tread down the rows, going over the rows lightly with the lawn rake when all the seeds are in. This deep planting prevents mildew, and the seed is less apt to be disturbed by moles.

The main crop of peas, which are grown through

the warmer months, may be planted to advantage on a heavier soil; they should be kept cultivated and free from weeds and the earth drawn up against the vines a couple of times before maturing. This is all the culture required, peas being one of the easiest vegetables to grow.

Here is a list of varieties that have been called "the Aristocrats" among peas. They are sure to perform as promised below, on the basis of many years of trials.

VARIETY NAME	50% READY AFTER	LAST PICKING DAYS LATER	HEIGHT OF PLANT	PODS AV. PER VINE	PODS LENGTH INCHES
Market Surprise	55 days	5	2½ feet	Five	4
Little Marvel	60 days	7	1½ feet	Eight	3
Sutton's Excelsior	62 days	4	1¾ feet	Six	4
Thomas Laxton	72 days	6	3 feet	Seven	4
Blue Bantam	78 days	6	1½ feet	Six	4
Alderman	80 days	8	5 feet	Eight	4½
Quite Content	84 days	6	5 feet	Eight	5½
Buttercup	87 days	6	2 feet	Six	4½
British Wonder	85 days	5	2 feet	Ten	3½
Potlach	86 days	8	2½ feet	Ten	4½
Dwarf Champion	88 days	7	3 feet	Seven	3½
Royal Salute	90 days	5	4 feet	Ten	4

OKRA

This vegetable is grown for the green pods which are used in soups, to which it imparts a rich gelatinous quality, and are as easily grown as peppers, requiring about the same culture. The seed should not be sown until the ground is warm—about the middle of May; it should be sown rather thickly in drills, three feet apart, sowing the seed an inch deep and thinning when large enough to stand ten inches apart in the rows.

The pods must be used while young and tender, as when fully grown they are very tough, though they may still be used to flavour soups.

Keep well hoed and free from weeds.

OKRA AS A VEGETABLE

Put the young and tender pods of long, white okra in salted boiling water in granite, porcelain, or a tin-lined saucepan, as contact with iron will blacken them; boil fifteen minutes, remove the stems, and serve with pepper, salt, butter, and, if preferred, vinegar.

PEPPERS

Are grown from seed started early in April in the hotbed or in flats in the house and planted out when all danger of frost is passed. They require rich, well-drained soil and a sunny situation. Where the supply of manure is limited, a spoonful of phosphate may be placed in each hill as the plants are set, and more be scattered about the plants and

THE GROWING OF VARIOUS VEGETABLES

hoed or raked in until the growth is satisfactory. Set out in rows two feet apart, setting the plants eighteen inches apart in the rows.

The culture that will produce good corn, cabbage, or tomatoes will be right for peppers, as they are of easy culture. Hen manure may be used with this plant, as it is one of the few plants which is not injured by the application of so strong a fertilizer.

The plants come into bearing in July, and if the first peppers are removed while green, the succeeding fruits will come forward more rapidly than if the peppers are allowed to ripen.

Chinese Giant, Magnum Dulce, and Sweet Spanish Giant are the best of the large sweet peppers, the latter being a long pepper, from two to three inches wide and six to eight long; this variety is rather more shapely for stuffed mangoes than the bull-nosed varieties. The large squat peppers are excellent for table use, being prepared in various ways.

Several of the hot and pickle varieties of peppers are both useful and ornamental, the Celestial or Christmas variety being especially ornamental. These may be grown in pots on the kitchen window and the fruit enjoyed throughout the winter. They are an attractive addition to pickled cauliflowers, onions, and the like.

The Tabasco is an especially beautiful pepper, bearing its fruit in sprays of brightest red, which are extremely fiery and pungent, and the seeds may be used for making pepper vinegar instead of the cayenne.

EGG-PLANT

This is one of the few vegetables requiring special care in cultivation. The seed should be started in a warm hotbed in April, and as soon as the plants are three inches high they should be potted off into small pots and plunged back into the soil of the beds. They may be transplanted into the open ground when the weather is quite settled and the soil and nights warm, or they may be repotted into larger pots and set out in the open ground the first of June.

Egg-plants require a great deal of heat at the start, and if they receive a setback at this time, rarely recover, so that every effort should be made to keep them from being chilled, while at the same time giving them the necessary amount of ventila-

THE GROWING OF VARIOUS VEGETABLES

tion. It is well in planting the seed of egg-plants to reserve a portion in case the first sowing should fail and a later one need to be made.

After the plants are of a size to be planted out there is little difference in the culture accorded them and that given other vegetables, but they should not be allowed to suffer for water, and a weekly dose of liquid manure after the plants bloom will be of benefit.

When about a foot high, the earth should be drawn up about the stem in cultivating. The plants are often seriously injured by the potato-bug, which eats the stem of the blossom at the point where it curves over, seldom, to any extent, the leaves of the plant. Whenever the bug appears early in the season, the plants should be gone over daily to catch and destroy it, or they may be sprayed with Paris green, which at this stage will do no harm. The destruction of these first blossoms will make two or three weeks' difference in the maturing of the first crop and must be met energetically. These first bugs which appear lay their eggs on the underside of the leaves, and these must be looked for and destroyed and little subsequent trouble will be experienced.

THE VEGETABLE GARDEN

Curiously enough, for a plant which starts out in life so peculiarly sensitive to cold, the egg-plant is not hurt by light fall frost, and I have gathered and marketed very fair eggs long after the frost had destroyed tomatoes and other garden stuff.

The best variety to raise is the Early Black Beauty or the Improved New York.

CHAPTER ELEVEN
ROOT VEGETABLES

Root crops are now generally considered just as essential to the welfare of our bodies during the winter months as are beans, corn, and peas during the summer months. Incidentally, while it is true that some of these root crops, like beets and carrots, are more tender if stored in cans rather than sand or soil, it cannot be denied that, in the process of canning, their valuable vitamine-carrying qualities are appreciably diminished. Hence, in suggesting varieties, I have been governed by their keeping qualities under cellar-storage conditions rather than by their suitability for canning purposes.

In connection with the root crops, Professor Osborne, of New Haven, Connecticut, is gladly given credit for the information that, according to their relative vitamine-carrying qualities, turnips rank first, carrots second, and beets last. Since kohlrabi and ruta-baga, or Swedish turnip, are members of the turnip family, it is safe to say that they have at least as much nutritive value.

As fifty per cent. of all Americans, regardless of class, are over-fed and under-nourished, and seventy-five per cent. of all diseases that attack the human body are directly or indirectly traceable to this cause, a more thorough knowledge of the nutritive value of the various vegetables would undoubtedly help us all to better health. In these statements I am sustained by a medical authority on the subject of nutrition, or rather mal-nutrition. The "tired feeling" that attacks many of us in late winter and early spring is evidence that our bodies are ill-nourished. And, since such symptoms are most prevalent during that season, it is obvious that, with all our steadily advancing knowledge of nutrition, we are not, as yet, fortifying ourselves sufficiently against winter.

The chief causes of ill-nourishment are a lack of a proper amount of vitamines and an abundance of roughage. Fat, carbohydrates and protein will sustain life. They are, however, not alone sufficient to cause the human engine to function to perfection. Roughage is needed to remove accu-

ROOT VEGETABLES

mulations of impurities; vitamines are the factor needed to create the strong red blood essential to disease resistance.

The preparation of the ground for root crops should be deep and thorough, and ploughing is preferable to spading. All weed roots which are not thoroughly buried by the plow and show above ground after dragging should be pulled out by hand and consigned to the compost heap. The ground should be disc-harrowed, dragged, and raked to as fine a condition as possible. I like to have the ground lie a few days after being prepared before planting, in order that it may settle somewhat, and if a rain follows the preparation, all the better. Land moist from rain will not need to be tramped down over the seed, as will be absolutely necessary in the case of dry soil.

As a general thing, root crops should not succeed each other, but be rotated with vine or leaf crops. Root crops leave nothing in the soil and take largely from it. Vines and other forms of vegetables leave a large proportion of the growth to be returned to the soil, and are, for this reason, less exhaustive of fertility. Of course this is not of as much moment on the limited area of the kitchen garden, whose fertility is easily maintained by the application of animal fertilizers and the humus from a compost heap.

BEETS

Sow beet seeds as early in the spring as the ground may be worked up fine and mellow. Light, well-enriched soil suits them best. The seed should be sown in drills, one foot apart, sowing the seed an inch deep and treading down the rows. When the plants are large enough, thin out to stand four to six inches apart in the rows; keep them free from weeds and the soil soft and mellow by frequent cultivations. If wanted for greens, sowings of seed may be made every two weeks up to the middle of August, or, if but an early crop of greens is wished, the ground may be used for late peas when the beets are out of the way.

The regulation packet will sow twenty feet of row. For a constant supply sow a fifteen foot row every week from the middle of April until August first. One ounce each of an early midseason and late sort provides enough beets throughout summer, fall and winter.

The well-balanced kitchen garden invariably holds an abundance of rootcrops which fortify the home against want of vitamines during the winter

Onions, such as these Yellow Globe Danvers, are easily grown from seeds in 100 days. Text tells how

ROOT VEGETABLES

VARIETY NAME	READY FOR USE	IN "FIT" CONDITION	NOTES
Eclipse	60 days	10 days	Tough when overgrown
Crosby's Improved Egyptian	62 days	15 days	Uniformly sweet while young
Detroit Dark Red	65 days	20 days	The ideal early beet for home gardens
Electric	65 days	28 days	Rapid grower of steady quality
Fireball	68 days	30 days	Always sweet, flavor hard to beat
Crimson Globe	70 days	20 days	Develops over a long season
Early Model	70 days	10 days	Stringy when over grown
Columbia	75 days	30 days	Ideal late beet for poor soil
Edward's Early	78 days	30 days	The ideal main crop sort
Black Red Ball	80 days	30 days	Good even after over grown

CARROTS

Are one of the economic vegetables, being not only exceedingly wholesome and toothsome, but, like the sweet corn, possess the advantage of being edible in root and top, the green tops being much relished by cows and horses, and the peelings and any surplus roots forming a most valuable addition to the winter ration of horse and cow. The juice of the yellow carrot, when expressed by grating the raw root and pressing the juice through a cloth, makes an excellent and harmless colour for butter, giving it the much-prized golden tint of early grass butter in the spring.

A good story is told of a mother who took an anemic daughter to a famous physician noted for his bluffness and brevity. A brief inspection, a briefer "claret," and a wave of the hand dismissed patient and subject. A month or six weeks later the mother returned accompanied by a blooming daughter, and at the physician's nod of approval, the mother, becoming loquacious, explained that she "gave them to her three times a day cooked and raw." "Raw!" exclaimed the physician in amazement. When it transpired that his brief directions of claret had been understood as carrots, and they had been liberally supplied with the result of perfect recovery, whether through the medium of faith or the medicinal qualities of the vegetable, remained a matter of individual experiment, but it is an item in favour of the carrots that they are of no uncertain tonic value to animals.

To grow carrots in perfection requires a rich, deep, sandy loam, thoroughly prepared and deeply cultivated. For an early crop, the seed should be sown in April or May in drills, one foot to fifteen inches apart, scattering the seeds as thinly and evenly in the rows as possible and tramping them down. For a late crop, the seed may be sown as late as July 1st. As soon as the plants are large enough, they should be thinned to stand four inches apart in the rows and must be kept clear of weeds and well cultivated. A little nitrate of soda

ROOT VEGETABLES

drilled into the soil along the rows will greatly hasten the growth, or the nitrate may be applied with a watering pot by dissolving it in water. Phosphate worked into the rows before sowing the seed is a help to rapid growth when the animal fertilizer is limited, but is not necessary in well-fertilized land. For table use, the varieties known as Oxheart, Chantenay, and Paris Forcing, all commonly classed as bunching carrots, should be selected. Danvers Half Long is a very smooth, attractive sort, and, if well cultivated and thinned sufficiently, will grow to large size and prove profitable for stock as well as for the table, as even when large they are never coarse.

ONIONS

The most practical manner of growing onions in the kitchen garden is by the use of sets, which may be set out early in spring in shallow drills twelve inches apart and the sets four inches apart in the drills. The ground must be deeply dug and thoroughly pulverized, and when the onions are up so they can be seen, hand weeding through the rows will be necessary. The hand-cultivator may be used to keep the space between the rows free from weeds.

Care must be taken not to allow the mature onions to form seed, as this will render them unfit for food, the seed stalk forming a woody centre in the onion, which resists all efforts to cook tender. By watching the plants and breaking off all blossom stalks as they form, the onions will remain fit for use when stored for the winter.

There are no onions, however, so tender and delicate for table use as those grown from seed, which may be sown in the open ground early in March or April and thinned out to stand three or four inches apart in the rows. Or they may at first be thinned to stand from one to two inches apart, and as soon as large enough for the table, use as young, green onions; every other onion may be removed, allowing the remainder to mature for winter use.

A method of culture we have found very satisfactory is to sow seed in drills in August in very finely prepared ground, which must be kept well cultivated and free of weeds. A mulch of straw or other coarse litter as protection during winter should be given after the setting in of cold weather, and this should be removed in spring. Seed sown at that season gives an abundance of early onions of the tenderest and best quality, and the entire crop may be gathered in time for another sowing of seed in the following August. Onions succeed well when grown year after year on the same ground, and when the bed is well cared for one or two years, it gets in excellent tilth and is easily kept free from weeds.

By sowing onion seed in frames and transplanting in April, onions of immense size may be produced, and the labour is not much greater than that required by planting in the open ground, thinning, and giving the necessary preliminary weeding. In setting the young onions, which are very small and tender, a shallow trench is dug and the plants laid against the side of it at intervals of four inches, the earth being then filled in and pressed down against them with the hoe. The table herewith gives the acknowledged leaders among onions for home and market garden.

AMERICAN ONIONS OF SPECIAL MERIT

One packet each of an early white, large early yellow and late red generally supplies all the onions for moderate use in an average family. A packet sows 25 feet of row which, *on good soil,* yields ½ bu. of ripe onions. An ounce of seed will sow 200 feet of row.

VARIETY NAME	BULBS DEVELOP FULLY IN	SHAPE OF CLASS	AVERAGE WEIGHT PER BULB (OUNCES)
White Portugal	110 days	Semi-round	4
Southport White Globe	120 days	Globe	5½
Flat Yellow Danvers	108 days	Semi-round	4½
Yellow Globe	116 days	Globe	6
Southport Yellow Globe	126 days	Globe	7½
Prize taker	135 days	Globe	7
Red Wethersfield	135 days	Semi-round	7½
Southport Red Globe	135 days	Globe	7½
Australian Brown	125 days	Semi-round	5½

THE EXHIBITION TYPE OF ONIONS AND THE MILD "BERMUDAS"

It is a queer fact that those varieties of onions which may be grown to extraordinary size are really not Bermuda onions at all, but certain types of Spanish onion. The Bermuda onions proper are small to medium sized flat bulbs, averaging not more than two and a half inches in diameter by one inch through. No amount of extra start can make them grow any larger because they are a very early variety, ripening within sixty days from the time seeds are sown. They are of three kinds, namely, the Bermuda Crystal Wax, a pure white bulb;

ROOT VEGETABLES

White Bermuda, a yellow skinned fellow; and Red Bermuda, the rosy-coloured companion of the other two. These Bermuda onions are notorious for their mildness and for their poor keeping qualities. There is one member of this type, however, originally from Italy, Giant White Italian Tripoli, which, after naturalization here, is called Mammoth Silver King. This is the giant variety of the pure white, flat onion; and if started under glass, it will grow to a weight of from two to three pounds.

However, even that variety is not as interesting a specimen of giant onion as the misnamed "Bermuda onions" which we see displayed on the fancy fruit stands throughout the country, and which are giant, globe-shaped, yellow-skinned fellows.

The original of this tribe was a European variety called Yellow Zittau Giant which in due time gravitated to America, and about twenty-five years ago, was introduced as American Prize-Taker. Just about the same time, the well known house of Vilmorin in France "discovered" a very much milder flavoured onion of yellow, globe-shaped type in Spain, cultivated it for a few years in France, and offered it then under the name of Giant Spanish. The late W. Atlee Burpee introduced this variety into America, and it subsequently won its place as Gigantic Gibraltar, differing from Prize-Taker in having a deeper green top, and proving more resistant to blight and mildew.

Subject as it was to considerable variation of soil, moisture, and weather conditions, this Gigantic Gibraltar in the process of better adapting itself to loamy and mucky soils became somewhat modified. This modified form is now offered by some people in the trade as Giant Denia onion.

In the meantime, working along entirely different lines, a prominent English seed concern, starting with Yellow Zittau Giant as a foundation stock, evolved that great exhibition onion called Ailsa Craig, which today plays a very important part in every vegetable exhibit on both sides of the Atlantic.

Summarizing the recognized varieties of onion that may be suitably grown for exhibition specimens, we therefore have:

(1) American Prize-Taker, practical for cultivation on the clay soils pretty generally throughout the country.

(2) Giant Denia, thriving perhaps best under

irrigation, and in sections having well drained soils and a high altitude, though it also does well on muck.

(3) Ailsa Craig, capable of the greatest growth of any, but by far the most exacting in regard to its conditions of growth. It does particularly well on the Pacific Coast; also on deep, heavy clays and on loamy soils.

PARSNIPS

Like the carrot, they are an ornamental feature of the garden and may be grown to edge rows or beds of other vegetables if desired; they should occupy a prominent position in the garden, as their growth is lower than most other garden crops, and the beauty of the fern-like leaves makes them attractive at all times. They have not the bright colour of the parsley, being much darker in foliage, but they offset that vegetable and contrast beautifully with the red foliage of the beets.

They are one of the earliest vegetables to be started in spring, and so are out of the way before the main crops must be gotten into the ground, which is a distinct advantage. The seed should be sown in drills, like the carrot, making the drills a little farther apart—about fifteen inches—and dropping the seed as evenly and sparsely in the rows as possible. The seed should be planted about one-half of an inch deep and the earth pressed down above it. The soil should be rich and deep and the after cultivation thorough and constant. As soon as the seed has germinated and the little plants large enough to distinguish, all weeds should be removed from between and each side of the rows, the cultivator taking care of those between the rows. When the plants are three or four inches high, thin out to stand six inches apart in the row. The plants pulled up may be used to plant additional rows or to fill in any vacant places in the present rows.

While the quality of the roots are much improved by leaving in the ground over winter, enough for immediate use may be stored in damp sand or earth in the cellar, or they may be dug and piled in pits in the ground and covered with a mound of earth and boards to shed rain, but the cellar will be found more convenient, as in case of severe weather it will be found almost as difficult to get into the heaps as to dig the roots from the open ground.

ROOT VEGETABLES

The best variety to plant is the Large Sugar or Hollow Crown, and one ounce of seed will plant one hundred feet of drill.

POTATOES

Growing potatoes in a back or in a typical suburban garden is usually not advised because it is urged that, given the same amount of space, other crops are apt to be more profitable. That is true if potatoes are not really "grown"; yet it is in fact possible almost any season, if you meet every requirement of this exacting crop—for it is exacting—and do your part in making conditions favourable, to dig hills where eight to fifteen smooth, high quality potatoes roll out. And then potatoes *are* worth while!

If you are planting only a few rows or a few bushels of seed it is most important that every potato has a record of high performance back of it, or in other words that it comes from good seed, of a variety suited to the locality and that it be planted free from disease and kept that way as far as possible. Irrespective of the variety, by all means get certified or hill selected potatoes for your seed, and be sure they are not potatoes merely sold for seed.

Many a grower has found that high prices are not always a reliable guide in buying seed stock.

There are a few outstanding varieties from which the gardener should select the *type* he wishes to plant. For cool, moist regions and a deep rich soil with plenty of rainfall and cool weather, Green Mountain for late planting will give large yields of the highest quality; for the early planting Irish Cobbler, a blocky white-skinned tuber, will prove admirable. Where the crop has to contend with hot, dry periods during the summer, nothing will give better results than some variety of the "Rural" group. Among these are to be found such common favourites as Rural New Yorker, Carmen No. 3, Sir Walter Raleigh, and Golden Petosky. Here, too, such early varieties as Early Ohio and Irish Cobbler will give general satisfaction. If a few of the earliest type are wanted, a row or two of Triumph will give edible potatoes a week or ten days before Irish Cobbler or Early Ohio.

After having located the potatoes for seed, and while waiting for winter to pass, it is well to select the place for the potato patch. A rich, loose, sandy loam will give best results. It should be full of organic matter. To make sure of this, if possible,

ROOT VEGETABLES

cover it during the winter with well rotted manure to a depth of two or three inches and plow or spade early in the spring, later thoroughly mixing up the soil and manure and working the soil just previous to planting to a depth of about eight inches. Thorough pulverizing of the soil will afford a loose plant bed, unlock the necessary plant food, and help to retain an abundance of moisture so necessary for big yields.

For early potatoes the earlier they can be planted the better, while the late ones can be planted from May until July, depending on the locality. When the tubers are dormant, preferably at least a month before planting, treat them for scab and other disease carried on the outside of the tubers. This consists in immersing the tubers in a solution of corrosive sublimate for an hour and a half, but no longer. Place the potatoes to be treated in a wooden barrel or other container and cover with the poison solution. The amount needed will vary with the quantity of potatoes to be treated, but an ounce of corrosive sublimate powder dissolved first in a quart of boiling water and then added to seven and one half gallons of water will be sufficient to treat a couple of bushels.

After soaking the tubers for an hour and a half take out and spread them out to dry. Potatoes so treated should never be eaten or used for stock food.

After treating, place them in a cool place and about three or four weeks before planting time spread them out on the floor of a room or crib where they will be exposed to the light each day. Of course they must not be allowed to freeze. In a short time the vigorous tubers will produce tough green sprouts which will grow about a quarter of an inch long and then cease growing. Tubers which produce fine spindling sprouts or none at all should be discarded. Green-sprouting potatoes in this manner will make early potatoes mature ten days earlier and give a more uniform vigorous stand. For late potatoes remove from storage and spread out in the light where they first begin to show signs of sprouting.

In cutting, the slice under the stem end should be cut off first, cutting about one half inch deep. Then examine the cut surface, if it is white it may be used for seed, but if it has dark spots in it, about a quarter inch under the skin, discard; for this is an indication of wilt, a common potato disease which

ROOT VEGETABLES

causes the early death of the plant. After making this initial cut the tubers should be cut into pieces about the size of a hen's egg with at least one green sprout to each piece.

It is best to plant immediately after cutting, one piece in a place in rows twenty to thirty inches apart, spacing the pieces about twelve inches distant in the row. For small gardens rows may be placed as close as eighteen inches. Cover the pieces from three to five inches deep and keep the soil loose over the patch until the growths appear. Level cultivation, all the time keeping a shallow dust mulch, will conserve the moisture and keep the plants growing vigorously.

When plants are eight inches tall spray them thoroughly with bordeaux into which lead arsenate has been placed. Bordeaux mixture is made in small quantities by dissolving three level tablespoonfuls of copper sulphate in about a quart of hot water and then pouring into a large jar or wooden bucket and adding sufficient water to make three quarts. Next mix ten level tablespoonfuls of hydrated lime with a quart of water and *pour into* the copper sulphate solution, stirring all the time. This is bordeaux ready for use. To con-

THE VEGETABLE GARDEN

trol the potato bugs stir into this quantity six level tablespoonfuls of powdered lead arsenate. To make larger quantities all that is necessary is to multiply the amounts of the various ingredients.

Bordeaux will stimulate the plants and keep them green and vigorous after unsprayed vines have died. When poison is added, potato bugs are controlled at the same time. At least three applications of bordeaux should be made, about ten days to two weeks apart, during the growing season. By thorough spraying, many Indiana farmers have secured from twenty-two to thirty-five bushels more potatoes per acre.

At digging time it is a wise gardener who goes into his patch and selects a few of the most vigorous hills with a large number of smooth uniform potatoes for his seed stock another year. These should be kept in a cool, moist place during the winter.

RADISHES

For very early use, the seed may be sown in hotbeds or frames and a second crop sown in the open ground, in a sunny, sheltered position, in April. The seed may be sown at intervals of two or three

The methods by which such "hills" of five-pound crops, as shown above, are grown, are fully described in accompanying chapters

Crisp, brittle delicacies that make your mouth water are easily grown in even smallest gardens

ROOT VEGETABLES

weeks up to the first of September. Sow in thoroughly prepared ground in shallow drills ten inches apart and thin to stand two inches apart in the rows, permitting, of course, more space for the larger summer and winter varieties.

There are three reasons why radishes grow "pithy", i. e.: (1) improper soil, (2) growing the wrong variety for a given season, (3) not thinning out.

First, as to the soil. The "ideal" for this particular vegetable is a well enriched loam, with a slight admixture of clay; one that is rich in humus and almost devoid of clay will grow as brittle and as handsome a radish as any one may want, but it will be practically tasteless. On the other hand, in a stiff clay devoid of humus the development of the radish will be so slow that it becomes woody or, during a sudden hot spell, spongy and pithy; and it also tends to make side roots.

For all practical purposes radishes may be divided into early, mid-season, and late sorts. Among the early varieties some of the best behaved are Rapid Red, Crimson Giant Forcing, Scarlet Globe, Sparkler, French Breakfast, Long Scarlet Short Top, and White Icicle. It is a peculiar fact that

THE VEGETABLE GARDEN

the handsomest radishes are also the ones showing the most fickle tendencies. Among those named, Sparkler (which is the finest strain of Scarlet Turnip White Tip), and French Breakfast, its olive-shaped companion, will become pithy much more quickly under contrary conditions of soil and season than any of the rest.

Long Scarlet Short Top has a white-tipped associate, Long Brightest Scarlet or Cardinal. Within the short period of twenty-four hours, on rich muck soil I have known this latter to turn from a perfect looking, though comparatively tasteless crop, to a pithy, useless one. So rapid is the deterioration of this variety that the growers themselves frequently are not aware that the perfectly good radishes they marketed yesterday are unfit for market to-day.

The varieties named, and in the order given, with fair soil and weather conditions, should become ready for use in from eighteen to twenty-five days, up to May 1st.

There are really only three varieties that deserve to be called heat-resisting, mid-season sorts. One is Chartier, or Shepherd, which is a long red radish, ready for pulling from July 1st to 15th from seeds sown May 1st to 15th. Other claims to the contrary notwithstanding, I have found Long White Vienna, or Lady Finger, no better than Icicle.

The other two varieties that will really stand heat are White Strasburg and White Stuttgart, both white-skinned, firm-fleshed, summer varieties, differing somewhat in shape and—though very little—in time of maturity. From seeds sown early in May they will give good returns during August, when every other variety goes on strike.

There are two distinct classes of the large-growing winter kinds: one that keeps well and one that does not. The Chinese varieties, of which White Chinese, or Celestial, and Chinese Rose Winter are the best-known, will grow woody or spongy after December 1st, no matter what soil produced them. On the other hand, the European varieties of the Spanish type will require longer to develop and will not grow so large, but will be firm-fleshed until away late into spring. Now just as there is a likelihood of planting early radishes too late so also may the mistake be made of planting the winter varieties too early! In the latitude of New York the best time is about July 1st to 15th; i. e., when you would sow winter turnips. An earlier sowing may yield a larger root, but not one fit for the table.

The last, though not the least important, point in radish growing is the need of proper thinning out and transplanting. Most home gardeners (and even professionals, for that matter) seem to forget that good radish seed, such as is sent out by every reliable seed house, grows better than 90 per cent. In consequence about *ten times as much seed* in a row as that row can hold in the way of well-developed radishes is usually sown.

Even when planted with the greatest precaution, every row of radishes will hold too many seedlings; and crowded rows, while not directly responsible for pithy roots, help a great deal to bring this condition about. Therefore, thin out determinedly; allow for the small round kinds one to two inches apart in the row; for the long and mid-season varieties, at least four inches apart in the row, six inches being better for both White Strasburg and White Stuttgart; winter radishes should be at least six inches apart; for the Chinese varieties, eight inches is better.

ROOT VEGETABLES

DEPENDABLE RADISHES FOR ALL SEASONS

One packet sows 30 feet of row. An ounce each of an extra early round and long white, plus a packet of a summer and winter variety, will provide for the whole year.

VARIETIES	FIRST ROOTS READY IN	50% READY DAYS LATER	SIZE OF TOPS WHEN OF EATABLE SIZE
Extra Early Scarlet Turnip	30 days	7 days	8–10 small leaves
White Box	32 days	10 days	large
Sparkler	27 days	6 days	6–8 medium leaves
Hailstone	24 days	5 days	6 small leaves
Snowball	25 days	5 days	6 small leaves
Rapid Red	22 days	4 days	4–6 small leaves
Crimson Giant Globe	26 days	7 days	8–10 large leaves
Vick's Scarlet Globe	31 days	10 days	8–10 large leaves
White Olive Shaped	25 days	7 days	6–8 small leaves
Scarlet Olive Shaped	25 days	9 days	6–8 medium leaves
French Breakfast	25 days	7 days	6 sm all leaves
Icicle	35 days	8 days	8–10 large leaves
Long Scarlet Short Top	40 days	5 days	8–10 large leaves
Cincinnati Market	40 days	10 days	8–10 large leaves
Lady Finger } Summer	42 days	10 days	big tops
Chartiers }	40 days	10 days	big tops
White Chinese or Celestial } Winter	67 days	72 days	large leaves and tops
Round Black Spanish }	75 days	90 days	med. leaves, large top

SALSIFY OR VEGETABLE OYSTER

Salisfy requires the same culture as carrots and parsnips. Sow early in spring in drills fifteen inches apart, scattering the seed an inch deep and treading down the rows. Thin to stand four to six inches apart in the rows and keep clear of weeds and the soil well worked and mellow. Salsify may

THE VEGETABLE GARDEN

be used in the fall or left in the ground over winter, being used early in spring, when it first appears in market. A supply for the winter may be dug and kept in boxes of moist earth or sand in the cellar if desired. When left in the ground, it should be dug before growth begins in the spring. It succeeds best in a light, mellow soil. The Mammoth Sandwich Island is the best variety to grow, Long White is also a good variety.

TURNIPS

Are usually grown as a catch crop to follow.after some other crop which has failed to prosper or has matured and been gathered. For winter use, they need not be sown before the middle of July or the first of August. Any good garden soil will grow the turnip, as it is not particular as to soil or location. For garden culture, the seed should be sown in shallow drills fifteen inches apart and the plants thinned to stand four to six inches apart in the row.

Popular sorts to grow, among the early kinds are Snowball, Purple Top Strap Leaf and Purple Top White Globe. The most widely planted among the better keeping winter sorts or Rutabagas is American Purple Top Yellow.

CHAPTER TWELVE
VINE VEGETABLES AND FRUITS

Though limited in number, the fruits or vegetables produced by plants of a viny nature comprise some of the most important and interesting of the garden's productions. The culture differs somewhat from that given other plants and is limited to a shorter period of active operations. All vine growths are exceedingly tender when young, and for this reason cannot be gotten into the ground until all danger of frost is past and the soil is warm. The seeds of this class of plants—especially of melons in variety—are very sensitive to wet or cold and prone to decay if conditions are not quite right. It is often, for this reason, necessary to repeat the planting twice or oftener before a good stand of plants is obtained. No seed should go into the ground at the North before the twentieth of May, and in many instances the first of June will give better results. Where very early fruit is desired, seed may be started in the house or hotbed by cutting sods from a meadow or other place and cutting them in squares about five inches in diameter and packing them closely together in a warm hotbed. The grass, if long, should be sheared away and the sods set grass-side down. On each of these pieces of sod five or six seeds of melons or squash may be planted, covered with two inches of rich, fine soil or manure, and when the seeds have germinated, all but three of the best may be removed. When the weather is favourable, these pieces of sod may be planted out in the open ground in hills prepared as for seed. Great care must be taken in handling the sods, as there is no plant grown in the garden so sensitive to disturbance in transplanting as the musk-melon. Cucumbers and squash are less sensitive, but even these will stand little disturbance and handling. Old strawberry baskets are sometimes used for this purpose, being placed in the hotbed close together and filled with rich soil well pressed into them; when transplanted, basket and all is removed to the field. Do not set them in the open until after June 1st.

A warm, sunny situation suits all vine plants, and a light, moist, sandy soil, heavily enriched with well-decayed manure, is necessary for their successful culture.

The ground should be very thoroughly prepared by deep ploughing and repeated dragging and raking. The seeds should be planted in hills four feet apart for cucumbers and six for muskmelons, while eight feet apart will give none too much room for squashes and water-melons. Two or three spadefuls of manure should be incorporated in each hill, which should be raised a little above the surface of the ground. The object in planting in these raised hills is that water may not settle about the plants should excessive rainfall follow the planting. In dry seasons level planting would be all right, but seeds planted on the level in a wet season will be quite certain to decay, and even plants which have come up will damp off under these conditions. Planting on elevated hills is a measure of protection which may be supplemented by covering the hills with a frame of wood or a light box with the bottom knocked out and replaced with a pane of glass; given this protection, the plants will come through a wet spell fairly well. In the small home garden the use of frames is a very practical and satisfactory measure, as after the plants have become started and the weather sufficiently warm, the glass may be replaced with a screen of window netting and the plants protected from the squash-bug or beetle, which creates such havoc in the melon patch.

These frames, if removed and stored in a dry place as soon as the need for them is over, will last for years. They should not be left on the hills after the vines have made enough growth to escape from them, and in the early stage of growth, while the glass is in use, it should be removed during the hottest part of the day and netting used to prevent burning, and to allow the plants the advantage of fresh air.

As soon as the plants have made a foot or less of growth the ends of all the branches should be pinched back. This encourages the plants to branch freely and will also result in the first blossoms formed setting fruit which will ripen much in advance of fruit on unpruned vines. It is claimed by some that the first blossoms set on the vines are sterile and would bear no fruit, but this is not my opinion, nor does experience justify any such theory, as I invariably find that when the vines are pinched back they produce from three to five

VINE VEGETABLES AND FRUITS

melons close to the root, which are always several days or weeks earlier than those on the remainder of the vines. I note this of the melons especially, squashes giving one or two fruits at the base of the plant.

Where ground is at a premium and one only desires to grow sufficient fruit for the private table, very satisfactory results may be obtained by growing the melons and cucumbers on netting. The hen park-fence affords an excellent opportunity for this form of culture, and I find that the hens do not disturb the vines in the least.

I do not think the vines produce quite so freely as on the ground, but the fruit matures quite as well, and the labour of caring for and gathering it is so much less than when grown on the ground, and the fruit so much more attractive in appearance, that the method has much to commend it. Cucumbers especially do well, and the fresh, bright appearance is in marked contrast to that of the ground-grown fruit. There is no labour connected with the growing of vegetables so trying as that of gathering pickles; the difficulty of getting about among the vines and the stooping position necessary to their gathering make it exceedingly wearisome. Where they are grown on the ground, it will be well to curtail the growth sufficiently by frequent pinchings back or directing the running vines, to allow room to pass between the hills without treading on the vines, which seriously injures them and stops their bearing.

Cultivation should begin about the hills as soon as the plants are above ground, and earlier if the soil becomes hard or caked. Some twelve or fifteen seeds should have been planted in each hill. This allows for those which decay or for any reason fail to start and furnish food for the bugs, which are quite sure to appear unless the plants are protected by frames. When the plants have gotten their rough leaves and the bugs have left them, all but three plants should be removed and these encouraged to grow by the application of a little nitrate of soda worked into the hills about the plants in the proportion of a tablespoonful to a hill. Hen manure is also an excellent dressing for this purpose.

If the trowel or light hoe is used about the plants in the hills and for a little distance out, no weeds will gain a foothold there, and the hand-cultivator will take care of the ground between the hills. Cul-

VINE VEGETABLES AND FRUITS

tivation should be continued as long as there is room enough between the hills for the cultivator to pass and should be followed by the rake to produce a clean surface and a dust mulch. When the cultivator can no longer be used, there will still be work for the narrow rake or hoe, and this should be used as long as possible. After the vines cover the ground they should not be disturbed further until the fruit begins to ripen.

In very dry and dusty spells of weather the vines may be watered with advantage, especially if the watering may be done with a hose, so as to thoroughly cleanse the vine, and liquid manure may occasionally be given with advantage.

CUCUMBERS

When wanted for pickles the cucumbers should be gathered as soon as they are large enough. It is better not to gather both pickles and cucumbers for the table from the same vine, as the maturing of the fruit decreases the production of young fruit. Often, however, there will be enough pickles overlooked in gathering to supply an average family with cucumbers for the table. It is always best to gather the tiny pickles first, depending for large pickles for use in making mixed pickles, pickled lilly, mangoes, and the like on the later fruit, as this keeps the vines in better bearing condition. Any fruit which has grown too large to use or has begun to ripen should be at once removed, as the production of seed will greatly exhaust the vine, and there is no economy in saving more than two or three for seed.

The fruits grown on vines trained on wire netting are so easily gathered and so easily found that the picking is apt to be much cleaner than where the vines are grown on the ground.

For growing on netting, the best variety is the Japanese Climbing cucumber. This is a fine, large variety of a rich dark green, and very shapely. It is a prolific bearer, and I find the flavour superior to any previously grown and it is exceedingly crisp and firm. It is equally good as a pickle or table variety. Perhaps the best all round sort for the home garden is Davis's Perfect, a handsome sort equalling in both quality and appearance, the finest hothouse product. Those desiring pickles in quantities should plant Boston Pickling or Snow's Perfection or any of the Early White Spine type.

VINE VEGETABLES AND FRUITS

MUSK MELONS

The introduction of many new early ripening kinds has extended the usefulness of the musk melon considerably. It may now be grown in sections having a minimum of 100 frostless nights. Planting in the garden should be delayed until all danger of frost is past—about the time for planting sweet corn—when the ground has become warm and moderately dry, is the proper time.

The most congenial soil for melons is a warm sandy loam, well worked and enriched with old compost. Plant in very slightly raised hills four to six feet apart each way; place the seeds about two inches apart, one inch deep and from eight to twelve in a hill. A shovelful of old compost or rotted manure should be placed in the bottom of each hill.

When the young plants form the third pair of seedling leaves, thin them out to three vigorous plants to a hill. Cut off the surplus plants just below the surface so as not to disturb the roots of those remaining. Keep the surface loose by shallow hoeing, but in no case disturb the roots, and never work the ground when the leaves are wet with dew or rain.

The best melons grown in the home garden are usually from seed sown in hotbed in pots or on inverted pieces of sod, the same as cucumbers. The sash should be removed only on clear, warm days, and never in cool or cloudy weather. Give plenty of ventilation, which is afforded by raising the sash about two inches about the frame. Keep the soil moist, but provided with good drainage. To prevent burning give the glass a light coating of oil and turpentine—one part oil to five parts of turpentine, or cover the frame with plant cloth. Earliest varieties are ready for the table in from ninety to one hundred days, and the general crop in from one hundred and fifteen to one hundred and forty days from planting the seed.

Among the many varieties we suggest the following for the home garden: Rocky Ford or Netted Gem, Emerald Gem, and Burrell's Gem or Salmon-fleshed Rocky Ford. Among the larger fruited sorts, particularly suitable for cool location, the following will serve admirably: Long Island, Beauty, Montreal Market, and Champion Market.

The White Spine type of Cucumbers provides fruits for both slicing and pickles. Early White Spine shown above

The fruit that made Rocky Ford famous from coast to coast and that helped to extend melon culture considerably

WATERMELONS

Cultivation is about the same as for musk melons, but differs mainly in that watermelons, being of larger and stronger growth, require to be planted a greater distance apart. To secure strong plants early in the season, place large, well drained hills from eight to ten feet apart, any time after Decoration Day.

When the soil is warm and comparatively dry plant from eight to twelve seeds to each hill, about three inches apart and from one to one and a half inches deep. Set the seeds edgewise with the eyes down. Two large shovelfuls of rotted manure or compost should be mixed with the soil of each hill and so worked in that there will be no injury to the young vines from quick drying under hot suns.

Protect the young plants from insects with netting or by the use of dry sifted ashes sprinkled over the leaves when wet; hasten growth by frequent applications of liquid manure. Thin out to from one to two strong plants to each hill. Early Fordhook is ready for the table in from ninety to one hundred days; the general crop in from one hundred and twenty to one hundred and forty days from planting the seed.

Among many good varieties suggested for the family garden, are Fordhook Early, Halbert Honey and Kleckley Sweets.

SQUASHES

Squash are such rank growing vegetables that they are especially benefited by liberal pinching back, and this should be done as soon as the vines are a few inches long and continued at intervals until cultivation ceases. There is little difference in the cultivation accorded the summer and winter squash. The varieties known as bush squash, however, are planted much closer together—from three to four feet, giving room enough for these. Where one has a convenient compost heap, sufficient summer squash may be grown on it to supply the needs of the table. They make a pleasing addition to the summer bill of fare, and some of them are good winter keepers.

For a winter squash there are no better varieties than the old-fashioned Hubbard and the Golden Hubbard, the latter being a much more prolific bearer and ripening its fruits much in advance of

VINE VEGETABLES AND FRUITS

the warted Hubbard. I do not think it is quite so good a keeper as the Hubbard; these we have had in perfection until mid-March, but so much depends upon the manner of handling the squash after harvesting that that must be taken into consideration in comparing any two varieties.

Any variety of squash must be gathered before they are injured by frost, but unless the shell is so hard as to resist the thumb nail, they will not prove good winter keepers, nor will they cook very dry and mealy, as a good squash should. Such squash should be used at once if for table use, but they will be much relished by the poultry should they be unfit for household use, and should be stored in as dry a place as possible and kept for that purpose.

PUMPKINS

Though generally considered a by-product of the corn field, quite a few pumpkins may be raised in the home corn patch. After the last cultivation of the corn, drop a few seeds in every third row or hill and let the vines run at will. Sweet Sugar is perhaps the most widely grown, while Winter Luxury (also known as Livingston's Pie squash) is unquestionably the highest quality pumpkin available.

CHAPTER THIRTEEN
GREENS AND SALAD VEGETABLES

The plants which are grown for their leaves which are eaten either cooked or raw form a healthful and important part of the garden's offerings. It is a question if any of the cooked vegetables afford so marked a relief from the winter bill of fare as does the dish of dandelion or other greens, which may be gathered wild by the dweller in country or village. Unfortunately, these wild things of the fields and woods are not so available to the dweller in towns and cities, but there are many cultivated vegetables which are very palatable substitutes for these and may be grown in the limited area of the back-yard garden. In the cities materials for salads may be obtained throughout the year; this is especially true of lettuce and celery salad, which is in the market most of the year.

GREENS AND SALAD VEGETABLES

CELERY

About middle of March, sow the seed in finely raked soil in a frame in drills four inches apart, and firm the soil well with a board. Give an abundance of water, and as soon as the plants are two inches high, transplant in other frames, in soil that has been enriched with a layer of manure, three inches deep, which has been thoroughly worked into the soil. Set the plants four inches apart, and do not plant too deeply. Firm the earth well about the roots, water thoroughly to settle the soil, and shade for a day or two, until the plants have taken root in the new soil. They will grow very fast and will need an abundance of water. The first sowings will be ready for the permanent position in the garden about July 1st.

Dig trenches fifteen inches wide and eight inches deep and four feet apart. Put about four inches of good cow manure in the bottom, tramping it down firmly. Add about two inches of soil to plant in, so that roots do not come in contact with the manure. Set out each plant with a good ball of earth, in double rows (which are about ten inches apart) and six inches apart in the row, taking care not to bury the heart. The best time to plant celery, unless the day be dull or there is a sign of rain, is in the afternoon after three o'clock, as the sun is then not so strong. From this on, the celery should be constantly watched, kept free from weeds and watered thoroughly and frequently if the weather is dry. For celery which is wanted for early use, earthing up is necessary about the middle of August. Pull the soil up to the plants with a hoe, breaking all lumps, gather the leaf-stalks tightly together with the left hand and press the soil closely around them with the right hand, using care to prevent the soil from falling into the heart of the plant, and thereby rotting it. Two earthings will suffice for Golden Self Blanching and White Plume. Then hemlock boards may be placed on edge on each side of the row and supported with stakes. This will help to blanch and whiten the celery. In this manner, White Plume and Golden Self Blanching will be ready for use September 15th. Giant Pascal is a late large celery and one of the very best flavoured varieties grown. It will be ready for use about December 1st. Another late variety, Fordhook Emperor, can be kept in trenches until May. Have the rows

GREENS AND SALAD VEGETABLES

of these late sorts about six feet apart, so that there may be sufficient earth to protect them during the winter.

WATER-CRESS

This is prized for salads and sandwiches, and grows wild along the margins of streams and about springs. Similar conditions may be supplied for a small patch of it by planting it about a hydrant from which water is allowed to trickle. Good soil, supplemented with a liberal addition of leaf-mould from the compost, should be supplied, and in this the cress seed may be sown in shallow drills a few inches apart. The only culture it will require after once getting started will be to keep it free from weeds.

Upland cress, which is more frequently grown in the home garden, is grown in shallow drills in beds, setting the rows a few inches apart and thinning the plants somewhat by using plants from too congested parts of the drills. Repeated sowings should be made at intervals, as the upland cress quickly forms seed and is no longer useful for the table. The Upland Cress and the Extra Curled or Peppergrass are the varieties commonly grown, while the Erfurt Water Cress is the variety favoured for this sort.

Very dainty sandwiches are made by buttering lightly slices of very thin bread, with the crust removed, salting slightly and placing sprigs of the cress between the slices. Only the newest, most tender leaves should be used for this purpose. Cress is also served as an appetizer, to be eaten with the fingers, accompanied with salt.

CORN SALAD

This unique and comparatively little known salad plant is much liked by some. It is sown early in spring in drills one foot apart. It is one of the quick-growing vegetables, maturing in about six to eight weeks. For winter and early spring use, sown in drills in August and September. It should be protected over winter by a light mulch of straw or litter.

ENDIVE

Is one of the best and most wholesome salads for fall and winter use. Sow in shallow drills in April for early use, or for late use, sowings may be made in June or July. When two or three inches high,

GREENS AND SALAD VEGETABLES

thin out to stand about a foot apart in the rows. The plants which are removed may be used to set other rows or to fill in any vacant places in the present rows. They should have mellow and very rich soil, as all salad vegetables require to make a quick growth in order that the leaves may be crisp and tender.

When they have nearly gotten their growth, the plants should be blanched by bringing the outer leaves together above the heart and tying with yarn raffia or bits of cloth strips, or anything which will not bruise the leaves. The tying must be done in dry weather, a clear, sunshiny day being best, or, like the cauliflower, the inner part of the plants will mildew or decay. Some growers cover the plants with boards or canvas, much as is done in the case of celery. It takes from three to four weeks to blanch the plants. Like all vegetables, it is necessary to keep the rows clear of weeds and well cultivated. Giant-fringed or Oyster endive, from seeds sown in the middle of May will yield average plants by the middle of August and, if shaded by either boards or muslin during the hottest part of the day, will supply salad material while fall lettuce is coming on.

KALE

Kale is cultivated the same as cabbage. It may be sown from May to June, one ounce of seed planting two hundred feet of drill. For early spring use, sow in September and protect during winter. A light frost improves kale.

LETTUCE THE YEAR AROUND

Five factors determine the degree of our success in growing lettuce: season, soil, moisture supply, strains of seeds, and cultivation. It is up to the planter's ingenuity to figure a way whereby the other four factors may be combined to work against the first (season) for the greatest results. Let us consider them in detail.

The first step is to put the soil in as good condition as possible for the crop, which is not difficult because as a group the salads are not particular. The one thing they *do* require is liberal quantities of quickly available plant food, especially humus. Humus is rotted vegetable matter and is to be incorporated into the surface soil. Fresh stable manure, dug under 6 to 8 inches, rye and other green crops, ploughed under to an equal depth, are

GREENS AND SALAD VEGETABLES

beyond the reach of the salad plants. They form humus in due time; but the salad plants must have it at once, and my experience is that it pays to work a generous supply of the commercial article right into the row. Rotted cow manure and well-rotted sod-soil serve the purpose equally well.

Strange to say, moisture supply, the next factor in success, is the least important under certain conditions of cultivation. I have raised finer heads of lettuce right on Long Island during July without irrigation than ever were produced with the help of watering. When the plants do not get moisture from above, they go down for it—if the soil texture is right. They then form long tap roots with few laterals. Surface irrigation, on the other hand, produced shorter tap roots with bunches of laterals; in a drought such plants quickly shoot up seedstalks even before heads are formed.

Strain of seed is a most important factor. Please note that I say *strain*. Ordinarily we would specify certain *varieties,* but in the case of lettuce we go farther. There are, for instance, two types of Tennisball lettuce—the White Seeded, with many variations; the Black Seeded, with fewer. Now, White Seeded Tennisball is like to a bucking bronco—you never know when it will bolt; yet nine out of ten seed catalogues still offer it, for antiquity's sake.

Black Seeded Tennisball, on the contrary, is the best of all the extra early Butter-head sorts for early spring work. May King and Wayahead, which I consider strains of Tennisball, are white seeded, but have characteristics of merit. May King will do well under meaner conditions of soil and season than any other extra early heading variety, while Wayahead is *the earliest,* though somewhat more exacting.

Amazing results may be scored with lettuce between the middle of April and the end of November, if only proper selections are made. It is essential to choose *a variety that will do its best at the period in which it is to be grown.* May King during May is a wonder; during July it is a joke. New York or Wonderful, during June, is a disgusting looking, flat, coarse plant; with the approach of hot weather in July it fortifies its interior by forming walls reinforced by strong midribs. With no other vegetable is the question of "specific strains and varieties for specific seasons" as all-important.

GREENS AND SALAD VEGETABLES

THE PROGRAMME OF SOWING AND THE KINDS TO SOW

I take it for granted that the gardener had access to a coldframe during early March in order to provide seedlings of Black Seeded Simpson. As an alternative, most seed and plant establishments are generally prepared during April to supply sturdy plants, suitable for transplanting into the open ground, 10 inches apart in rows, 18 inches between the rows. Where this can be done *early in April,* the gardener will enjoy crisp lettuce from early in May until the middle of June. But please remember Black Seeded Simpson is *not* a "head" lettuce.

As soon as the ground can be dug and raked (generally about April 15th) sow short rows each of Wayahead, May King, Black Seeded Tennisball, and California Cream Butter. When thinning these, about May 5th to 10th, transplant the sturdiest seedlings wherever there is space in the garden. These four varieties will mature in succession, supplying salad from the middle of June until the middle of July, when California Cream Butter will "bolt" to seedstalks.

THE VEGETABLE GARDEN

The *first week in May* sow All Seasons, Iceberg, New York or Wonderful, and Kingsholm Cos. This will provide heads from early July until early August. While thinning the seedlings of New York or Wonderful, transplant the sturdiest, which will be ready about a week later than those left to grow in the original row. By the middle of August, even Kingsholm Cos will go on a strike; and from then on, for about four weeks be satisfied to do without lettuce. But endive sown in May will supply the salads for that interval.

Early in August sow a row each of Unrivaled, Crisp-as-Ice, and New York or Wonderful. These will provide salad from the middle of September, when Unrivaled will be ready, until Thanksgiving when the last of New York or Wonderful may be snowed under.

At this time the coldframe will help again. By the *middle of October,* transplant a score each of Crisp-as-Ice and Wonderful into the frame, covering the plants during severely cold nights, and you may enjoy fresh lettuce of your own growing even up to Christmas, depending entirely upon the severity of the season.

GREENS AND SALAD VEGETABLES

CARING FOR THE GROWING CROP

The least understood and therefore least practised detail in lettuce culture, the lack of attention which is responsible for 75 per cent. of all failures (balance to be credited to choice of poor strains), is thinning the growing crop. The seedlings *must be thinned* to give ample room for the unhampered development of the individual plant. Do the first "thinning" (which is really cultivation) when the plants are just large enough to be taken hold of, generally 3 to 4 inches. Lettuce seeds germinate from 90 per cent. to 100 per cent. Everyone sows them too thickly. The result is crowded rows, spindly seedlings, a war of "the survival of the fittest," a waste of plant food on the unfit, and permanent injury to the crop.

Thin out so that every lettuce stands at first 4 inches from its fellow in the row. As soon as the little plants fill that space, remove every other one, now fit for salads. Repeat this thinning out process until the plants stand 12 to 18 inches apart, the small varieties requiring less room, the larger ones as much as 2 feet of space for each head in the row.

THE VEGETABLE GARDEN

From the time that the little plants become individuals on a street rather than babies in a crowded tenement, the hoe or any cultivator should be kept busy. Besides hoeing both sides of the row, stir the soil *in the row,* between the plants. No other vegetable crop I know responds so thoroughly to diligent and thorough cultivation. It will grow fairly well even in soil poor in humus, so long as frequent cultivation is practised, and will stand a surprising amount of drought.

UTILITIES OF THE DIFFERENT CLASSES

There are three distinct branches of the lettuce family, each of specific usefulness at different seasons: (1) the Looseleaf class, members of which will *never* form heads; (2) the true Head lettuce; (3) the Cos lettuce which forms upright bunches of leaves, folding more or less tightly, according to variety.

The first is important only for very early work; it will thrive in lower temperatures, and meaner weather, and get along on poorer soil than any other type. But that's all that can be said in favour. Neither in quality nor in appearance do

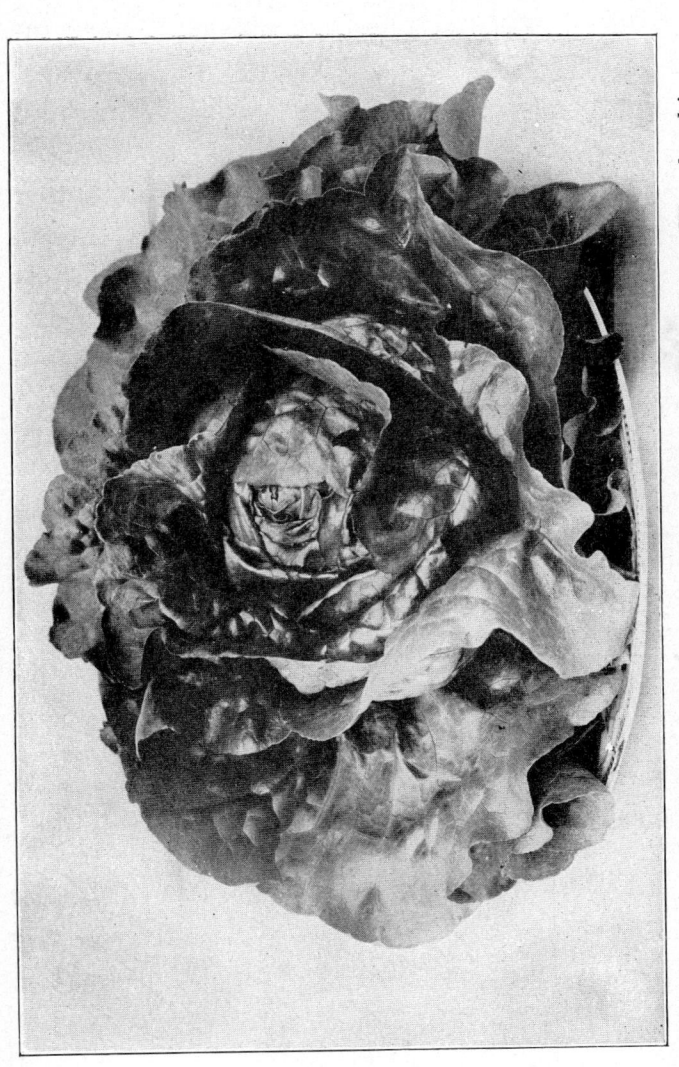

Nothing comes up to the "butterhead" type in quality and among them Wayahead is way ahead in every respect

The Chinese have sent us many queer things, but the usefulness of Chinese Cabbage as a salad has been firmly established

they measure up to the other classes. The most important of the early Looseleaf type is Black Seeded Simpson. Prizehead—a poor name for a sort that won't head, and positively misleading—ranks second.

Among the Cos lettuces, the chief value of which lies in their heat resistance, Express or Eclipse is the earliest, but small. Paris White grows larger, does well during early August and is of better quality. Kingsholm is the largest and latest of the three and while of a rather forbidding appearance, it holds a heart of gold.

Head lettuces, however, are the ambition of every home gardener. They are of two kinds: Butterhead and Crisp-head.

The Butter-heads are distinct from the others in having leaves of markedly delicate texture which seem oily or buttery to the touch. The Crisp-heads lack this characteristic, forming strongly ribbed heads which somewhat resemble small cabbage, wherefore they are called "Cabbagehead" in some catalogues. The Butter-heads carry off the quality prize, they are best served with French dressing, whereas Crisp-heads are often given a bacon fat dressing.

THE VEGETABLE GARDEN

But there is reason for growing both **Butter-heads** and **Crisp-heads** in the home garden. When the best of the Butter-heads wilt and go to seed under August suns, the Crisp-heads, with their tightly folded heads and strong midribs, prolong the salad season for another week or ten days, perhaps.

For perfect succession of delicious Butter-head lettuces, use the following varieties (the figure after each name indicates the time required to form heads from the time of sowing seeds):

Butter-heads: Wayahead (45); May King (50); Black Seeded Tennisball (55); California Cream Butter (65); All Seasons (75).

Crisp-heads: Iceberg (70); Hanson (75); New York or Wonderful (80).

Crisp-as-Ice is difficult to classify; with Butter-head quality its growth character is Crisp-head. It is the one variety, however, I prefer to all others for late season work. It will stand a remarkable amount of cold weather without injury.

OTHER WORTH-WHILE SALADS

Chinese Cabbage is better as a salad than as a cooked dish. Do not sow until early in August

GREENS AND SALAD VEGETABLES

and its development will be most rapid, so that by late September, and from that on until snow covers the ground, you can count on gathering delightful, crinkled, well blanched heads, weighing from two to five pounds each. The flavour of this salad is delightfully pungent.

Witloof Chicory is for connoisseurs among salad eaters. This is the French Endive of Europe. Seeds are sown early in April, the plants making a strong growth throughout the season, and the roots are dug in the fall. The tops are then cut back to within an inch of the neck, the roots are shortened at the bottom so that all are a uniform length of from six to eight inches. They are then packed upright in deep boxes, the crowns covered with sand, soil, or moss. After watering, place in a warm cellar. If this be done in the middle of November, a delightful crisp, aromatic salad will be had at Christmas.

MUSTARD

Is one of the most satisfactory vegetables used for greens. It is also used in combination with cress as a salad. The seed of both the black and white mustard is quite universally used in pickles of various kinds.

For salad use, it is sown thickly in shallow drills about six inches apart, forming beds of the drills. It should be sown at intervals during the summer to assure a succession of new and tender growth. For early spring use, it may be sown in frames or boxes, where it can be kept from severe cold. Keep free from weeds and cultivate sufficiently to keep the soil open and soft.

In using mustard for salads or greens only the leaves are used, and these should be carefully washed and looked over that no grit or insects may be included in the cooking. Cook like spinach in an open vessel until done, drain through a colander, pressing free from moisture, and serve seasoned with salt, pepper, and melted butter.

SPINACH

Is one of our most important vegetables, and should be found growing in every garden. The culture is simple: the chief point to bear in mind is that it requires very rich soil; it can scarcely be too rich, as upon its rapid growth depends its succulence and tenderness. For spring and summer

GREENS AND SALAD VEGETABLES

use the seed is sown in shallow drills, a foot apart and one inch deep, as early as the ground can be worked in the spring and every two weeks thereafter for a succession. For winter and early spring use, sow in well-worked and manured ground in September, covering the plants from frost with straw at the approach of severe weather.

The Round-seeded Savoy is one of the best varieties for summer use, but the new Victoria is said to stand the warm weather somewhat better and to be in many respects an ideal spinach. The New Zealand variety is a large-growing variety, and is usually planted in hills three feet apart each way. One ounce of seed will plant a hundred feet of drill. Keep free from weeds and well cultivated, watering freely in dry weather.

CHAPTER FOURTEEN
PERENNIAL VEGETABLES

THE list of perennial vegetables commonly grown in the kitchen garden is not large, but it includes some of the most indispensable vegetables of the kitchen cuisine. They come into use so early in the spring that they provide fresh vegetables at a time when the palate is most jaded from a winter diet and bridge over the period of waiting for the new planting to become productive.

ASPARAGUS

Is the most palatable of our spring vegetables and comes into cutting in May. The usual way of starting an asparagus bed is by setting out the roots, which are obtained of the florist or market gardener; but very excellent, though somewhat slower, results follow the planting of seed. In growing the asparagus from seed, the usual way is to plant the seed in drills in rows one foot apart in thor-

PERENNIAL VEGETABLES

oughly pulverized and well-manured ground. The plants must be kept entirely free from weeds, and to achieve this it will be necessary to do considerable hand work, pulling out the weeds from between the plants and loosening up the soil with the fingers. The young asparagus plants are very slender and fragile, and thus close culture and weeding is essential. As soon as the plants are a few inches high, they should be thinned out to stand six inches apart, and from that on be cultivated sufficiently to keep the soil mellow and entirely free from weeds.

The second spring the young plants may be transplanted into permanent beds, which should be so located as not to be in the way of the cultivation of other parts of the garden. It will be found that setting the rows far enough apart to cultivate between will greatly advance the culture and lessen the care.

The ground for the permanent beds should be very rich or specially prepared. The rows should, if they are to be cultivated by the hand-cultivator, be not less than eighteen inches apart and the plants set a foot apart in the rows; this will enable the gardener to cultivate each way of the plants and will produce fuller stools of asparagus and larger shoots than if the plants are set closer together.

In preparing the ground for the plants, it should be trenched to a depth of eighteen or twenty inches, several inches of rich manure worked into the bottom of the trench, and the plants set in this. Sufficient earth should be filled in about the roots to cover them three inches deep, more soil to be added in cultivating after the plants are set. Place the roots in a natural position, rounding up the soil somewhat under the crown and spreading out the roots; press down the earth firmly about them and level all off gradually in cultivating.

Thorough culture may be given the first year, or resort may be had to a mulch of straw, marsh hay, or lawn clippings, which will greatly reduce the care of the beds, and if sufficient material is used, keep the beds in quite satisfactory condition.

As soon as the plants have become old enough to bear berries I prefer to cut the fruiting tops before the seed shall have ripened and burn them, replacing with other litter; but this should not be done till the tops have quite matured. I find that allowing the old plants to seed will, in a short time, produce a crop of young plants which, unless re-

PERENNIAL VEGETABLES

lentlessly treated as weeds, choke out the old plants, and are troublesome to destroy and altogether undesirable.

Cutting for use may begin the second season, but should not be carried to the extent that would be practised on an old bed, and should be discontinued while yet the roots are throwing large, healthy shoots. In cutting asparagus for use, it should be cut just below the surface, never very much under it, as all that grows below the surface is tough and unfit for use. Where the bed is not producing sufficient for use at first, it may be gathered from day to day and placed upright in a dish of water until sufficient has accumulated for use. It will, in this way, make considerable growth and the flavour will not be very much impaired.

As soon as the bed has come into bearing it should have all the rough litter removed very early in the spring and a liberal top dressing of wood ashes and fresh manure spread over it. Nitrate of soda and other commercial fertilisers may be applied at this time or deferred until the roughest of the manure is removed preparatory to cutting. Salt is often applied in the proportion of six hundred pounds per acre, or about four pounds to the square rod, but it is not a plant food and only serves as a weed killer for a very short time. If one wishes very early asparagus, one should plant it in rows running east and west and with a sunny southern exposure and protected on the north by a high wall or building. A rough board frame around the beds, covered with sash, may be provided and this well banked with rough litter during winter. In February this is removed and the frames filled with fresh manure, which should also be banked about the outside of the frames. Part of the inside manure will need to be removed as soon as growth begins and the sashes lifted during the warmer part of the day to admit air. As soon as the weather becomes warm the sash and frames may be removed and the beds given the usual treatment.

Asparagus is successfully forced in warm cellars by lifting clumps of roots in the fall and placing them on the floor of the cellar, as is done with rhubarb. It is, of course, necessary that the plants become frozen for some time before forcing and that the cellar be warm and dark, or that light should be shut away from the immediate vicinity of the plants by turning boxes or barrels over

PERENNIAL VEGETABLES

them. A position back of a furnace offers a favourable position, as it is usually out of the way, warm, and not too light. Here, on the cement bottom of the cellar, a bed of rough boards or a big shallow box, adapted to the purpose, may be prepared, and the roots, which must be lifted before the ground freezes, but left outside to freeze, covered with loose earth until some time in November or December, when they are set closely together therein. Sufficient earth should be added to cover the crowns of the plants, and this may be well enriched with manure. It should be kept moist, for it will be remembered that the asparagus is a plant of the spring, when the earth teems with moisture. If the cellar is at all light, it will be necessary to cover the beds with a frame of wood, covered with canvas, old carpet, or anything convenient, or even a heavy mulching of straw. This is not actually necessary after growth has begun and the shoots are breaking ground. Additional heat may be provided by placing a lantern under the frame and covering the beds. Barr's Mammoth, Conover's Colossal and Giant Argenteuil are three sorts of proven merit, equally useful in all sections.

THE VEGETABLE GARDEN

RHUBARB

Is much appreciated by many in the early days of spring, and has certainly much to recommend it as a tonic and appetiser. There are few gardens in which a root or two of rhubarb will not be found growing, so accommodating is it as to environment and conditions, but it is, at the same time, a plant which will well repay liberal culture. It should be given a permanent position in a warm, sunny place, and the ground should be very deeply dug, as the plants make an immense root growth, and the hole in which it is set should be dug eighteen inches or two feet deep, and all poor soil at the bottom should be removed and the excavation filled in with old manure and good, mellow soil. On this the roots of the rhubarb should be set, the crown only a little below the surface of the ground. The ground should slope away from the plants to insure good drainage in the winter. Cultivation in the early spring should be given, but will not be necessary throughout the summer if a mulch is placed over the ground on each side of the plant. The great overhanging leaves are quite effectual discouragers of weeds, and few, if any,

PERENNIAL VEGETABLES

will grow in the immediate neighbourhood of the root.

A heavy mulch of rough litter should be applied about the plants in the fall, and in the spring half barrels or boxes may be turned over the plants and fresh manure packed about them; this will much advance the growth of the plants. Later, as the weather grows warm, this may be removed and the plants allowed to make a natural growth, but the use of the barrels acts as a forcing house for early stalks.

Rhubarb is easily forced in a warm cellar. The roots should be dug before the ground freezes and left outside, lightly covered with soil and brought into the cellar after they have been severely frozen. For the best results, however, this should not be done until about Christmas time, it will force better then. A dark, warm cellar is necessary, and where there is a heating plant, the furnace room will afford an excellent location for their forcing, or roots may be placed on the ground under the hot water or steam pipes, where they run under the floors of rooms under which there is no cellar. If a strip or two of wood is nailed to the floor above the pipes, to which a heavy piece of duck or canvas can be secured to extend down to the earth beneath, it will form an enclosure for the plants, which will retain heat and shut out light effectually. It will also be a convenient place in which to attend to them if the pipes are near the cellar wall. The soil in which the plants are set should cover the crowns several inches and should be kept moist—not wet— and any suspicion of mould or mustiness should be counteracted by airing as needed. Rhubarb grown in this way is very tender and delicate. Old rhubarb plants in the garden or field should be dug up, divided, and plants with only two or three buds be replanted in very rich soil every three or four years. No insects are injurious to the rhubarb.

HORSE-RADISH

May be grown in any out-of-the-way corner, but seems to prefer a rather low, damp place. It is one of the most easily propagated of plants, as it thrives best when most disturbed. A small piece of the root stuck in the ground will quickly strike and commence to grow. It is not necessary that the crown of the plant should be used, a piece broken some distance below the crown doing equally as

PERENNIAL VEGETABLES

well and often better. It is for this reason difficult to eradicate once it has become established.

This persistence in growth makes it convenient for use, as a few roots may be dug up and placed in a crock of water and will continue to grow and furnish a pungent relish for weeks. It is only necessary to see that the water is changed occasionally, so that it does not become slimy, and horseradish will be at hand for immediate use without the trouble of going to the garden and digging it up each time it is wanted. It is one of the easiest of vegetables for winter forcing, as a few roots can be taken up and placed in a box of moist earth in a light cellar and will continue to grow all winter.

This ease of culture and survival under unfavourable circumstances indicate that it will spread rapidly, but this does not seem to be one of its faults, as a patch of it increases its boundaries but slowly, and there is little fear of its overrunning the garden to any extent. The leaves are of much use in sickness as a blister, and the plant itself highly ornamental.

Horse-radish, when grated for the table, should be mixed with white-wine vinegar, never with cider vinegar, as this gives it an unpleasant, dirty colour.

PARSLEY

Is one of the most useful of our perennial vegetables; it enters into all forms of savoury cooking, either as a seasoning or as a garnish. It is almost as appetising as cress for a sandwich, and gives an air to the plainest dish when used as a garnish. Strangely enough, its use seems little known outside the cities, and is regarded rather as a curiosity than a necessity by many. It is easily established in any spare nook, or may be used to border beds of flowers or vegetables.

The usual manner of starting a bed of parsley is by sowing the seed; the plants may be transplanted, but will not do as well as the seed-grown plants.

The ground should be thoroughly prepared by spading and enriching, and the seed should be sown as early in the spring as the ground can be worked, as after the ground becomes at all warm or dry, the seed will not germinate. It may be sown broadcast or in drills a foot apart, covering the seed about half an inch deep, pressing the soil down firmly. When the plants are up, thin out to stand six inches apart in the rows. Keep clear of weeds

The well-stocked mid-summer garden holds an abundance of every kind of vegetable. Tomatoes, Swiss Chard and Beans shown here

Carrots easily rank among the most profitable root crops, while their foliage is quite ornamental. Variety Amsterdam Forcing shown here is one of the best for early outdoor work

PERENNIAL VEGETABLES

and well cultivated. In using the parsley, the leaves are picked and the crown of the plant left undisturbed. If allowed to go to seed it injures the plant for garnishing, but a few plants should be allowed to seed, as it propagates itself in this way and insures a succession of young and tender plants. A light covering of brush or evergreen boughs during winter will be of benefit. A few plants may be lifted and wintered in a light window of the cellar or in a kitchen window and will furnish leaves for garnishing throughout the winter.

Dried parsley is much used with other pot herbs in soups, and is easily prepared by picking the leaves and enclosing them in paper bags and hanging them in a dry, airy place to dry. Parsley was much esteemed by the ancients, who believed it prevented intoxication by absorbing the fumes of wine. It was much used, therefore, as wreaths and chaplets at their feasts and drinking bouts. It was parsley which Hercules selected for his first garlands of victory, and the ancients utilized the plants in their merrymaking and rejoicing; so, too, it was brought into use in their funeral decorations, sprigs of the herb being strewn over their dead.

CHAPTER FIFTEEN
THE MIDSUMMER GARDEN

If fortune is kind and gives you a little patch of ground around your summer cottage or bungalow, be grateful and set that ground to work. The food situation throughout the country is such as to make it eminently desirable to produce something wherever a piece of ground is available. And contrary to common opinion there is much that a garden may produce within the sixty days which spells the life of the average vacationist's garden, although the list of available varieties is of course somewhat restricted and includes only vegetables having a short season of growth.

Please remember that everything depends upon getting the seeds to sprout promptly, and then *keeping the plants growing* constantly. Therefore:

(*a*) Cover the seeds slightly deeper than you would early in the spring, and bring the soil in firm contact with them.

THE MIDSUMMER GARDEN

(*b*) After seeds are sown, should the natural water supply be inadequate, give the garden a *good soaking* with the hose or a sprinkling can.

(*c*) As soon as the seedlings appear, start hoeing; and be sure to thin them to four inches apart in the row so that crowding does not check their development.

Foremost among vegetables for which the vacation season is sufficient are beets, carrots, kohlrabi, and turnips.

Beets that will perfect a two-inch product within fifty days under favourable conditions are Crosby's Egyptian, Detroit Dark Red, and Eclipse. The young beets which you gather at the end of the sixty day period are about the finest product imaginable for the purpose of canning. In connection with all the root crops, it may be worth remembering that the canned product is far more palatable than the coarse grained full-grown crop harvested later and stored in soil for use during the winter.

Carrots of French Forcing and Golden Ball varieties are small but delicious. These should be used when the roots which are round are not more than an inch to an inch and a half in diameter. And as it takes a good many carrots of this size to make a meal, be sure to sow enough. Within forty-five days of sowing seeds Oxheart will grow nearly two inches in diameter by three inches long while, if you have full sixty days before you forsake your vacation garden, you may sow Chantenay or Model, the largest, also latest, of the really early.

Kohlrabi reaches the two-inch diameter size under favourable conditions in an amazingly short time. Experiment with so-called forcing strains of Early White Vienna Kohlrabi has convinced me that this vegetable may be gathered within fifty days from the time seeds are sown.

Turnips there are that will be ready in fifty days, but do not expect quick-growing varieties to keep well. Early White Milan sown the first week in July will be ready for use the second week in August and ten days later will come Purple Top White Globe. Neither of these will stay in fit condition very long however since August heat soon causes them to get bitter. For winter use, the Swedish Turnips or Ruta-Bagas are much preferable, since they have flesh of much firmer texture. However, American Purple Top will be ready for gathering the last week in September from seeds

THE MIDSUMMER GARDEN

sown early in July, when the product may be stored like Potatoes, and will keep as well.

Radishes there are of course—the little round Scarlet Button, Scarlet Globe, and Hailstone type which will be ready for table use within twenty-five to thirty days after sowing. Remember that these small kinds must be used as soon as they reach a half-inch size or a little larger. They will not stand any heat, and very quickly become pithy. A somewhat preferable variety is Icicle which, like Long White Vienna, grows to larger size without becoming hot and spongy, especially if the soil is full of humus. Of the two, Long White Vienna remains in good table condition about a week or ten days longer than Icicle, but it also requires a week longer (or at least forty days), before it reaches suitable table size.

Salad of several kinds may be gathered in the vacationist's garden, if varieties of lettuce that have proven reasonably heat resistent are sown. The best types are the Crisp-heads and the Cos (also called Romaine) varieties. Among the Crisp-heads, New York, or Wonderful (Los Angeles Market) will require all of sixty days to reach full size, but it will be found to be the hardest-heading of them all. Crisp-as-Ice is a very much smaller variety of rather forbidding bronze green appearance, but with a heart as golden and sweet as any lettuce grown earlier in the season. Crisp-as-Ice is the Crisp-head companion of Mignonette, a little Butter-head variety that has the reputation of standing more heat than any other in its class.

Among the Cos lettuces, Eclipse or Express is the first to be ready for use, but it does not stand very long before it "bolts" to seed. A better selection would probably be either Paris White Cos or Dwarf White-heart Cos, both of which bleach to a splendid white inside and remain in good condition for the best part of two weeks after reaching table size.

Greens are provided liberally by the New Zealand spinach which is ready to begin cutting within forty-five to fifty days from time seeds are sown, provided the seeds are soaked in warm water for twenty-four hours before they are sown, and the ground liberally enriched with well rotted manure. For unless great quantities of quickly available food are put within its reach, New Zealand spinach will require seventy-five days to reach the cutting size.

THE MIDSUMMER GARDEN

Swiss chard is another prolific yielder of palatable greens, ready for cutting within fifty days from the time seeds are sown, providing those are soaked over night, sowed thinly in a well prepared row, and covered about one-half inch deep. After covering, walk over the row to press the soil in firm contact with the seeds. Then, after a day or two, get busy with the hose or sprinkling can, and give the ground a good soaking. Nature provides the heat and sunshine during July and August, but in order to have those two do the most good, man has to augment the frequently lacking moisture supply. Every vegetable will respond to regular watering, providing the watering is made more than just a sprinkling of the top. Give a good substantial soaking twice a week.

CHAPTER SIXTEEN
STORING VEGETABLES IN WINTER

VEGETABLES, which have been grown to perfection during the summer months and gathered while at their best, will deteriorate rapidly unless proper care is exercised in storing them away for the winter. Many of the methods employed by market gardeners and on farms where large quantities of fruit and vegetables are grown, and must be stored for sale at a time when they will bring a price much in advance of that which will prevail in the fall and early winter, are not practicable in the small home garden.

Any dry, frost-proof cellar will keep potatoes in good condition providing the precaution is observed of airing the cellar regularly and persistently. The most common mistake in storing fruit and vegetables in the cellar of the house is in the direction of too much heat and too little air. It is rarely that the cellar windows require to be closed

STORING VEGETABLES IN WINTER

before December, but in many cases they will be hermetically sealed at the approach of the first hard frost. This is not only bad for the contents of the cellar, but far worse for the people who dwell above the cellar. Where there is a heating plant in the cellar it is essential that there should be vegetable rooms separate from that devoted to furnace or boiler, and where this does not exist, an end of the cellar, at least, should be partitioned off for the purpose, though it may be but by a rough board partition; this as well as anything will shut out heat. Such a room should include one or more of the cellar windows, and preferably those on the sunny side of the house.

For the storing of potatoes there is no better arrangement than bins made long and narrow and with partitions through the centres, making compartments which will hold from one to three bushels of potatoes. There should be a number of large auger holes in the bottom of each and the bins should be elevated on some sort of supports to a foot or more from the floor. It must be remembered that cold falls and that the bottom of the cellar is much the coldest part of it, and where there is danger of frost, the floor of the cellar is

THE VEGETABLE GARDEN

the very poorest place in which to place anything that is to be kept from frost.

Potatoes should be dug on a bright day, when the soil is dry, so that the earth will shake off easily. Vegetables should never be washed before putting away for the winter, as they will not keep as well if they have been wet. Potatoes should never lie for any time exposed to the light, as this will cause them to turn green, and when they are placed in the cellar, should be kept covered with canvas, carpet, or newspapers, but carpet is best.

By the middle of winter it will be necessary to look the potato bins over carefully and to remove any tubers which may have begun to decay. One decaying tuber will produce thousands of fungus spores, which will contaminate the entire contents of the bins if not promptly removed. By the first of March, or even in February, the potatoes will have begun to sprout; especially will this be the case if the cellar is too warm and at all damp. They must then be gone over and all the sprouts rubbed off by hand.

If the cellar is quite dry, a portion of the potato bins may be reserved for the onions, which require a cool, dry place to be kept dormant in. No great

STORING VEGETABLES IN WINTER

amount of these will be stored for the winter use of a small family, and such of these as begin growth before being used may be planted out in the garden early in spring and will soon furnish messes of green onions for the table.

Squashes are one of the most difficult of vegetables to keep, as they are very susceptible to cold and moisture and must be kept warm and dry. An upstair room or garret will often be found an excellent place of storage. A room where a chimney passes through will often furnish sufficient heat, and if the squash are packed in barrels of dry leaves, excelsior, or buckwheat chaff, they will winter all right. Or they may, if few, be simply piled on the floor near the chimney and covered well with rugs, carpets, or something warm, and will usually come through all right.

Beets, parsnips, carrots, and turnips, on the contrary, need to be kept somewhat moist, and should be buried in damp earth, sand, or leaves. If one has a room in the cellar with earth walls and floors —what is known as a Michigan cellar—it will be an ideal place for these vegetables, and they may be simply piled in heaps on the floor and sufficient earth to cover thrown over them. This is the sim-

THE VEGETABLE GARDEN

plest form of winter storage for these vegetables. The earth is right at hand and needs neither to be carried out nor brought in. In storing the beets and carrots, I usually leave the tops on and pile one layer on the floor, the tops all one way, and place over them a layer of earth, then another layer of vegetables and more earth, and so on, until the lot is covered. The presence of the tops make uncovering the roots less difficult, and I think helps to retain a certain amount of freshness in the vegetable. Turnips are always prepared by removing all but about an inch of the tops and piling the earth over them. Treated in this way, they will all keep fresh and crisp until spring. Slightly moistened leaves make admirable covering for vegetables and are much cleaner than soil and more easily used.

Celery should be planted in boxes of damp sand or earth, drawing the earth up about the stems, as in the garden. Stored in this way, at a temperature of about 33°, it will keep fresh and crisp for a long time and be well blanched. Cauliflowers which have failed to mature their heads in the fall may be taken up and planted in shallow boxes of soil in the lightest part of the cellar and watered oc-

STORING VEGETABLES IN WINTER

casionally and will then mature their heads and be a welcome addition to the winter bill of fare.

Dry beans should be stored in a dry place—an upstair closet or cupboard—until wanted. They are not injured by freezing, and if more convenient, may be left in the barn till wanted. Salsify may be stored in damp sand, leaves, or soil, and a winter's supply of parsnips may have the same treatment, the main crop being left in the ground to be dug early in spring ere yet they have started to grow. Light is not necessary to plants stored in earth in the cellar, but sufficient air should be admitted to the cellar to prevent any musty or mouldy odours or taste being communicated to the vegetables.

Where the cellar affords little or no room for storage, enough for immediate use may be placed in boxes of earth or sand and the remainder cached in the garden. To do this, it is only necessary to dig a shallow pit and pile the vegetables therein and bank earth over them. Only enough to cover them completely should be placed at first, but more should be added at the approach of severe weather and the whole covered with boards to shed rain. Placing straw over the vegetables before adding the dirt makes them a little easier to unearth when wanted, but does not make them keep any better. Of course, if the heap is a large one, it will be necessary to provide ventilation, and this may be done by placing a length or two of old stovepipe in the centre of the heap and letting one end extend outside, where it should be masked with enough straw to shut out the cold but not to impede ventilation. Cabbages are very successfully kept by storing heads downward in a trench in which straw has been placed for a few inches in the bottom and covered up with earth above the tips of the roots and the ridge covered with boards to shed rain. A hotbed makes a very good place for storing cabbage, as it can be gotten into readily at any time during the winter. The earth should be removed as for fitting the bed in the spring; a layer of clean straw placed down on the bottom. The cabbages which have been pulled—not cut—are placed head down on this and the heads covered with earth; the remainder of the pit should be filled with straw or leaves to keep out the cold and the sash placed in position. Stored in this way, it is only necessary to reach down into the litter and pull out a head as wanted.

CHAPTER SEVENTEEN

THE CONSTRUCTION AND CARE OF HOT-BEDS, COLDFRAMES, AND PITS

To attempt to garden without the aid of a well-equipped and constructed hotbed is to put one at a disadvantage in the beginning of the season—a disadvantage which strenuous effort and the most favourable of seasons will rarely compensate one for, as a well-stocked and successful hotbed will supply the garden with an immense amount of plants of the most desirable varieties at the minimum of cost and at just the season that they will be needed.

The possession of a hotbed greatly advances the garden season, as the seed may be planted and the plants brought to a suitable size for planting out by the time that, lacking this convenience, the seed would be going into the open ground. This advances the season some six weeks, and makes an appreciable difference in the maturing of plants and vegetables.

THE VEGETABLE GARDEN

There has long been a feeling among the uninitiated that hotbeds, coldframes, and the like are conveniences reserved for the professional florist, the fortunate few who possess a gardener, or are otherwise favoured by fortune. Nothing could be more mistaken than this idea. The construction and care of the hotbed is so simple and, in its simpler forms, so inexpensive as to be within the reach of the gardener whose little plot of land comprises but a few square yards of ground, while at the same time its capacity may be extended to meet the requirements of the most extensive estate or commercial plant.

Primarily, it consists of a receptacle where bottom heat can be supplied and plants grown at a time when the weather is too cold for the carrying on of gardening operations in the open ground; where protection may be supplied against the elements and the conditions governing plant growth held in control.

The manner in which this is done will depend largely upon the length of the purse, the results will be the same whether it be a small hotbed or a large one.

There is so much questionable information floating around in the magazines and papers anent the

The well-stocked frame serves as insurance for early crops and against late frosts

Straw mat for use in very cold weather

proper time for starting the hotbed that a little discussion on this point may not be amiss at this time. I noticed an article recently in which it was stated that the middle of February was the proper time in which to start the hotbed. I have no doubt that there are certain sections of the country in which the hotbed may, with advantage, be started as early as February, but they will not be found in the vicinity of New York, Chicago, Detroit, or anywhere much north of Philadelphia. There is no amount of heating material which may be put into a hotbed pit, or any devised covering which will keep the frost out of a hotbed when the temperature is loafing around in the vicinity of zero for a stretch of several days at a time, as it is prone to do in February at the North. Nor would there be any practical reason for this early starting of the beds were it possible for them to be kept free from frost and the plants in a growing condition, which the necessity of covering with rags and things which shut out air and light for days at a time, would render impossible.

The prime object in the use of a hotbed is to have plants ready for setting out in the open ground as soon as the weather is favourable; this will not be, in the case of most plants, until all danger of frost is passed. This period varies according to location; in the vicinity of Detroit and Chicago it may be generally calculated as from April 1st to about May 20th, and throughout the country at large it may be generally accepted as the average "corn-planting time." Such seeds as radishes, beets, onions for transplanting, celery, etc., should be planted as soon as April 1st, and plants of cabbage, lettuce, etc., should be ready to go into the open ground by April 20th. It will then be seen that it is necessary to start the hotbeds early enough to get the plants sufficiently advanced to plant out when the right season has come.

Seeds of some plants require much less time to germinate than do others, and such seeds may be planted nearer corn-planting time than the others. Generally speaking, about six weeks, or at the most two months, should be allowed for the development of the plant; so if we accept May 20th as a safe time for this operation, it will be seen that the first of March, and not much earlier, is a good and practical time for getting the hotbed in commission. And very satisfactory results may be se-

CONSTRUCTION AND CARE OF HOTBEDS

cured by starting as late as the first or even the middle of April, as at that time the weather is mild enough for the sash to be raised a considerable part of the day, giving the plants abundance of fresh air, which makes for robust plants.

Plants which are left in the hotbeds even a few days longer than necessary are apt to be injured. For one thing, they become crowded and spindly, and their roots penetrate below the soil into the crude, heated manure and are injured; they become matted and must be separated, and more or less injury results in the process, all of which would be avoided if the plants could go into the ground as soon as they are ready.

Next in importance in the starting of the hotbed is the location; this will depend largely upon the arrangement of the grounds and buildings, and I can only point out the most desirable conditions.

The location should be the warmest at command and one which will receive the greatest amount of sunshine. It should be on the south side of a building or high-board fence, and should have some protection from rough west winds if possible. It should be easily accessible from the house, as the beds will require frequent and often sudden attention.

The lay of the land should afford good drainage, so that the water will not settle back against the beds; this is of special importance where the beds are to be used as coldframes for the carrying of plants through the winter.

Where the drainage is at all faulty it will be well to construct a drain in one corner of the beds by digging a hole and setting a porous tile therein, or filling with broken crocks, gravel, or other rough material. The opening should be flush with the surface of the soil, or slightly lower, and be covered with sphagnum moss or a piece of sod, laid grass-side down, to prevent the soil working in and filling the drain. This will carry off any surface water that might accidentally find its way into the beds.

But where the hotbeds are to be used the year round and may be considered permanent constructions, it will be well to begin right by draining the land in the immediate vicinity, if low, or by hauling on sufficient earth to raise the grade above the danger line. Considerable more soil will be thrown out in the first excavation of the pits than will be returned when the beds are made. All the subsoil removed may be used to raise the grade of the land if necessary, and where the same site is used for the beds from year to year, the handling of the soil as it is thrown in each year will aid in raising the soil in the vicinity of the beds, until in time a good natural drainage is established.

The construction of the hotbed may be of any building material, ranging from the inexpensive frame contrived from the waste lumber about the place and old window sash to florist's sash and walls of concrete, brick, and cement blocks, the last three being permanent and highly satisfactory. These permanent frames are the cheapest in the end.

For the temporary home or the small city lot, where it is desired to use the ground for other purposes, once the hotbed has served its purpose, the frame construction will be preferable; in the latter case it may consist merely of a frame set on the surface of the ground and removed when its usefulness is past; this forms the cheapest and also the least satisfactory of beds, for, while it answers the practical purposes of a hotbed, there is nothing below the surface of the ground to protect the beds from the incursions of vermin of various kinds—as mice and moles, two mischievous enemies of the hotbed and coldframe.

The size of the beds will depend upon the size of the sash used. If the frame is to be of plank and the sash discarded window sash, which, by the way, is by no means to be despised, the beds will be of a size to correspond. It will always be found an advantage in constructing hotbeds, especially if the beds are set against a building and are only to be approached from one side, to have them of a size that may be easily reached across, as nothing is more tiresome and unsatisfactory than to try to care for a bed too wide to be easily reached in all of its parts. Three feet will be as wide as can be conveniently handled, but the length may be as long as desired.

In excavating the pit for the frames it will be found a convenience, where there are several sash, for the pit to be in one long excavation, the necessary divisions being made by partitions in the frame itself, and which need not extend below the surface of the ground; these partitions, being removable, may be lifted in the spring, when the beds are to be made, leaving the full size of the

CONSTRUCTION AND CARE OF HOTBEDS

pit to work in, and will be found to require far less labour than to attempt the excavation of a number of small pits in restricted quarters.

The pit should be about four feet deep and of a size to readily receive the frame, and the sides of the pit should be as firm and even as may be practicable; the bottom, especially, should be level and hard, but no artificial bottom is required or should be made. In constructing the frame, four corner posts, of any rough stuff, two by four inches in diameter and long enough to reach from the top of the frame to the bottom of the pit, should be used, the posts for the back being six inches longer than those for the front. Upon these the planks, which should be of good size and of clear lumber that is free from knot-holes, or, if these cannot be avoided, they should be masked with pieces of tin nailed over them, so as to effectually shut out vermin of all kinds. The planks should extend below the surface of the ground two feet six inches according to the season, though, if preferred, they may extend to the bottom of the pit; but this is not really necessary, as moles, and especially mice, rarely enter beds at a lower depth.

The proper slant may be given the top by sawing a nine-inch board in two on the bias and using one section for an end, placing the boards with the sawn side down and nailing through the thin ends of the pieces into the boards below and also upon the corner posts. The frame should extend above the ground about a foot in the front and a foot and a half at the back. This gives the proper slant to shed rain, and also gathers the greatest possible amount of sunshine.

The back of the frame should be the thickness of the sash higher than the sides and front, if the beds are set close to a building or wall, in order that the sash may fit back snugly against the back of the frame, where they may be attached by hinges and so raised without removing. A notched stick should be fastened at the front or sides of the frames to hold the sash at any desired height when airing them. Where two or more sash are used and it may be desired to divide the bed with partitions in order that plants requiring different conditions of temperature, air, or moisture may be successfully grown, narrow strips of wood may be nailed to the back and front of the partitions at the point where the sash meet, and about an inch and a quarter apart; into these inch boards may

CONSTRUCTION AND CARE OF HOTBEDS

be slipped, their tops level with the sash and their lower sides extending slightly below the level of the ground; the top board will, of course, need to be sawed on the same slant as the ends of the frame. These not only serve the purpose of separating the several portions of the bed, but also furnish a firm support for the sides of the sash and of closing any cracks that may exist in the jointure of the sash.

All sash should be in a good water-tight condition, and no cracked glass or defective putty should be tolerated. It will be well if the amateur gardener acquaint himself with the use of putty, and so provide against the loss, by sudden breakage of glass by hail, carelessness, or other causes, of a valuable lot of plants. There are few things more prone to disaster than hotbed sash, and it might be helpful to know in this connection that broken glass is easily and quickly removed by the application of hot iron to the putty.

Where the ground is to be used for other purposes in the summer it will only be necessary to construct a frame about a foot high in front and eighteen inches at the back, with corner posts of equal height, as in this case the frame merely rests upon the surface of the ground, or only six inches or a foot below it, the soil and manure being piled about the frame to exclude cold. Such frames are very handy to protect beds of tender roses and other plants during winter, as they may be readily moved about from place to place, or if only wanted for spring use, they may be fastened together with pegs or hooks, and so taken apart and piled away like boards until wanted again another spring.

In constructing permanent beds with brick walls, the pit should be dug four inches larger all around to allow for the laying of the brick. Four inches—the width of the brick—will be sufficient for these walls, except where frost works into it, and second-class brick may be used; it should be laid with cement and given a finishing coat of one to three cement all over. In laying brick or cement walls it will be well to mortise in a strip of wood on the top for the sash to rest upon, also the cleats of wood for the partitions to slide in, and a shoulder may be left in the cement for strips of wood to extend across the beds under the jointure of the sash, to rest in, where partitions are not to be run through the beds and but two sash are to be used. Where window sash is used, it may be hinged to the strips of wood on top of the walls, as is done on wooden frames.

Concrete makes a very substantial and comparatively cheap wall. These should be somewhat thicker than the brick, and are laid up by the aid of a square wooden frame or form the size of the inside dimension of the pit, the excavation being about eight inches larger all around. In laying the wall, a rough concrete of sharp sand and gravel, in the proportion of one part of cement to six or seven parts of sand and gravel, is used. This is placed in the space between the frame and wall and tamped down firmly and until the moisture rises to the surface; all four walls may be laid at once to a height of one foot and then allowed to harden before adding the succeeding foot; always wet the last course of cement before adding fresh concrete. After the wall is built up to the desired height, a frame of narrow strips of wood should be fitted to the top, as in the case of the brick wall. Such a wall is very economical, warm, and durable.

Having constructed the hotbed of the chosen material, all that remains to do is to put it in commission. To accomplish this, fresh horse manure sufficient to fill the beds quite to the top will be required. This should be procured before frozen from that which has accumulated over night from young, grain-fed horses. It should be mixed with straw or, better still, with leaves—an amount equal in bulk to the manure. This admixture of leaves or straw is very important, as this furnishes heat by the fermentation or heating of the manure and insures the permanency of the heat; were only manure used, the heat would be intense at the start, but soon die out for lack of fuel.

The manure and leaves should be thoroughly mixed, and may be piled at once in the pits, packing it down lightly that all parts of the pit may be filled, or it may be allowed to get well heated before filling the frames. Should the manure be very dry it may be sprinkled with hot water. Place the sash on the beds and leave the manure to heat, which will begin almost at once if the manure is all right. The temperature of the mass may be tested by a thermometer thrust into it, or if a pitchfork is thrust into the manure and allowed to remain a few moments and then withdrawn, it will show at once if the mass is heating. When the heat has penetrated every part of the mass, especially the corners, it may be tramped down. Pro-

CONSTRUCTION AND CARE OF HOTBEDS

fessional gardeners put the manure in a pile and turn it over once or twice as it heats before placing it in the pits, but they handle so large a quantity that it is not possible to get sufficient at one time for all the beds, so older manure is used and allowed to heat in piles. For the home garden, however, I have found this way more satisfactory and far less work. Occasionally, when not able to get sufficient fresh manure for all my beds, I have supplemented it with manure from the heap at the barn, which had begun to heat, and have found it answered very well.

When the temperature has risen to a hundred degrees or more the mass should be tramped down as firmly and evenly as possible and an inch or two of old manure, made very fine, placed on top of it. Over this place four or five inches of good soil, composed of garden loam, leaf mould, and a little sharp sand well mixed. The surface soil should be entirely free from all rough matter, stones, roots, and the like, and to secure this condition, it will be well to pass it through a sand sieve or coal-ash sieve.

When the heat has begun to subside, so that the thermometer indicates ninety or less, the seed may be sown. The soil should be moist, not wet or dry, and if for any reason it should be wet, it must be turned over and over and dried out until in a condition to use; if too dry, it may be watered with warm water from the sprinkler of the watering pot and then allowed to lie under the sash until the moisture is uniform. Soil which adheres to the trowel in working is too wet to plant. It should fall apart after being pressed in the hand, not form into a ball or lump.

Before sowing the various seeds it will be well to obtain a supply of narrow strips of wood, which may be used to divide the various plats of seed from each other, by sinking them half way into the ground between the different sowings of seed. This is of moment, especially where more than one variety of different kinds of plants are sown—as cauliflower, cabbage, or tomatoes. Where but one kind of seed is sown in a sash, or one cabbage and tomatoes, for instance, in which there can be no difficulty in distinguishing them, it will not be necessary; still the presence of these little barriers prevents the washing of fine seed when the plats are watered, and defines the boundaries of the plats. When one lives in the vicinity of a

CONSTRUCTION AND CARE OF HOTBEDS

box factory, long, thin, narrow strips of wood admirable for this purpose can be secured. These make excellent labels, also, and should be prepared in advance of the time of planting. Not only the name of the seed should appear on these, but also the date of sowing and, where known, the period of germination. It is also well, where seeds of different seedsmen are used, to put the name or initials of the seedsman on the label. In this way one can judge of the relative value of the seeds, particularly if one is buying in large quantities.

In planting the seed, it is necessary to consider carefully the requirements of the various plants, and give those requiring a considerable amount of heat a sash by themselves, which the partitions under each sash will make possible, and place those requiring less heat and more air by themselves.

In gardening on a large scale, separate hotbeds should be used, and they should be started at different times to accommodate the requirements of the different plants; but in the small home garden this is not practicable, for even one small bed, three by six feet, may, by the use of a partition, be used to start a variety of vegetables at the same time with very fair success.

Egg-plants, peppers, and tomatoes may be started under the same sash, the cabbage and cauliflowers occupying the other sash.

When the date at which the various seeds germinate is known, it will be well to plant those which germinate at the same time in the same part of the frame for convenience in handling. It is also well to plant those seeds which make the more robust plants in the rear of the beds, that they may not overshadow the remaining plants, though there is less danger of this in the vegetable frames than in the flower frames.

Before beginning the sowing it will be well to provide one's self with a thin piece of wood, with a handle on one side to be used for pressing the seed into the soil. This is better than to try to pack it down with the hand, as it leaves a uniform pressure and a level surface. The board may be of any convenient size, but one about a foot long and ten inches wide will be convenient.

It is immaterial whether the seeds be sown broadcast or in drills; broadcasting requires rather less room, but plants in drills are more easily lifted and transplanted, and, where there is sufficient room, by placing the drills three or four inches apart, it

To get the most out of every tomato plant, it should be staked and pruned. The waste due to growing crop on the ground runs as high as 30%

This shows the "suckers" that thrive at the expense of the clusters, on every plant. Remove them at the leaf joints, throughout the season

CONSTRUCTION AND CARE OF HOTBEDS

will be possible to transplant half of the plants in the drills into fresh rows between the drills, a process which will produce much better plants. However, it is easier to scatter seed thinly when sowing it broadcast than in drills, and there is not so much danger of crowding.

Seeds sown under the protecting care of the hotbed do not need to be covered as deeply as when sown in the open ground, as they are protected from all changes of the weather, drying winds, burning sun, and washing rains. If well covered and the soil pressed firmly over them, that will be all that is really necessary in the matter of planting. An eighth of an inch of covering will be as much as such seeds as tomatoes, cabbages, and cauliflowers require, providing they are never allowed to dry out. Egg-plants may be planted at the same time as peppers and tomatoes, but the same temperature required for these would be rather high for cabbage and cauliflower were it not for the fact that by careful airing and shading of the beds these last can be kept at a much lower temperature than the former.

Both egg-plants and peppers germinate very slowly. Especially is this the case when the temperature of the hotbed is not sufficiently high, and much care is required to so regulate the sash as to afford sufficient air without at the same time unduly lowering the temperature. When all the seeds are sown, pressed down, and labelled, the soil should be sprayed lightly with a rubber sprinkler or the fine rose of a watering pot, covered with newspapers, the sashes closed, and the seed left to germinate. The beds must be examined every day to note if the soil is becoming dry, in which case it must be watered carefully as before, or if too wet and moisture gathers on the glass, the sash must be raised a little to allow the excessive moisture to pass off.

When the first plat of seeds germinates and the tiny green leaves appear above the soil, the paper should be lifted from that much of the bed and placed on top of the glass, directly over the plat. This shields the plants from the direct rays of the sun, while allowing sufficient light to reach the plants indirectly for their proper growth at this stage.

Many seeds have a tendency to come into the world heels up, and unless this penchant is corrected by turning the youngsters over into the soil, by making a tiny depression in the soil beside them with the point of a pencil to receive them, they are quite likely to perish. For this reason it is necessary to keep a close watch on the seedlings during the period of germination. The same end may be accomplished by sifting a little fine sandy soil over the seeds when they begin to germinate.

It is doubtful if any portion of the summer gardening is of greater interest than this watching of the breaking of the earth crust and the appearance of the tiny, tender green heads, and if good seed has been used and the planting carefully done, each square will present a mosaic of vigorous growth from the start.

The hotbed must not be neglected during these early days of growth, as sudden changes of weather may cause untold disaster. The temperature in a closed bed, under the influence of a bright sun, rises rapidly and the beds dry out with amazing frequency, and it will be necessary to admit air and exclude, to some extent, the sun by placing papers over the glass and raising the sash a trifle for the escape of the surplus heat. If, however, there is also a wind, it will be necessary to guard the opening on the windward side by a bit of rug

THE VEGETABLE GARDEN

or old carpet that no chill wind may blow over the exposed plants. Should the sun go under a cloud when the sash is open and the temperature fall, the sash must be closed at once. It will also be best to keep the sash closed during rains and lowery weather.

One of the most serious difficulties which confront the gardener in the management of a hotbed arises from a spell of hot weather when the plants are yet in their seed leaf, or the first week or two of growth; when this occurs to the extent of necessitating the closing of the beds for days at a time, especially if it also becomes necessary to protect the beds from the cold with rugs, not only shutting out the air but the light as well, then the situation is indeed serious, as there is often much loss of plants from damping off. The only palliative treatment is to watch the weather and not water the beds, especially at night, when a spell of wet weather is imminent; if the beds go into bad weather in fairly dry condition they will come through in much better shape. It is, for this reason, always better to water early in the morning if conditions are favourable.

The beds should be well protected with rugs or

mats on cold and frosty nights; glass radiates heat very rapidly after the sun goes down, and should, for that reason, in the early days of spring, be covered while yet it retains the heat. Whatever covering is used should be brought down well over the sides of the beds, and in windy weather should be held in place with racks or strips of wood. Shutters or some waterproof covering is necessary over the rugs in wet weather, as wet rugs or frozen ones do not exclude cold, and for this reason should be kept dry.

As the weather grows warmer and the plants increase in size, more air and sun should be given and the sash may be partially raised throughout the warmer part of the day. If the sun is hot, newspapers should be placed over the sash or the glass whitewashed. Later the sash may be removed during the heat of the day and replaced with lath screens, and as the season for removing the plants to the open ground approaches, these, too, may be dispensed with and the plants given full exposure to harden them off and make the plants grow more stocky.

Where there is room for it, much benefit will be derived from transplanting the plants, when they have grown large enough to handle, into fresh rows or other hotbeds. Such plants as cabbage, cauliflower, and lettuce may be transplanted into coldframes or beds in the open ground, where they can be protected with canvas in case of sudden drop of temperature, and grown on until time for transferring to permanent positions in the garden.

COLDFRAMES AND PITS

The coldframe is simply a frame of boards provided with sash or other protective material, and differs from the hotbed principally in that it has no heating material or pit beneath it, but is set on the surface of the ground. It has many uses and is a valuable adjunct to the garden. In the small home garden it is most useful for starting early lettuce, for growing a few melons or cucumbers ahead of the outdoor crop, or for carrying lettuce and cauliflower through the winter in order to have an early crop of these. It is also useful for wintering plants of artichoke, which will not endure the winter in the open ground at the North. It is a very useful auxiliary of the hotbed when used for transplanting the plants from those beds in order to give more room to develop. A very

CONSTRUCTION AND CARE OF HOTBEDS

small hotbed can be made to do service for a good-sized garden if supplemented by a coldframe.

The transplanting of any plant is a distinct advantage, as it not only allows of greater top development, but the root development is also much improved, as a new growth of roots is induced with each removal; and the greater the amount of roots carried by the plant when it goes into the open ground, the better will be its development and subsequent growth.

Any spent hotbed may be used as a coldframe through the summer and winter, and makes the best of places for the midsummer starting of pansy seeds and other flower perennials that are to be carried over the winter under sash.

It is well in constructing coldframes for winter use exclusively to build them so that they may be taken apart if necessary and stored away during summer. This may be done by making the four sides separately and fastening them together with pegs, hinges, or hooks; the joints should be a perfect fit, though, as the exclusion of cold is the first reason for their construction.

Where the coldframe is intended for the protection of any large number of plants, as in the

THE VEGETABLE GARDEN

flower garden, where beds of roses, azaleas, rhododendrons, and the like are to be protected, the span-roofed frame is preferable. This, as its name indicates, has a double sash or roof of glass and glass ends, being built with a wooden base a foot high all around and a frame about two feet high in the centre on which the sash rests, the gable ends being filled with glass. This is much more pretentious than the common coldframe or hotbed and much more commodious. It is not necessarily prohibitively expensive, and will more than pay for itself in the protection it affords.

The permanent hotbeds may be made useful and attractive during the summer by using them for planting out tropical plants or those requiring an unusual amount of heat and nourishment, as their location in the sunniest position furnishes the one and the great amount of manure they contain the other. No better place could be found for growing banana plants, whose luxuriant growth requires just these conditions. It will also be found a convenience in applying water, as the frame and the lowness of the soil inside prevent all waste, and the soil can be kept wet under conditions that would be impossible in the open ground.

CONSTRUCTION AND CARE OF HOTBEDS

The space back of and between the wall and hotbed may be utilised for the growing of vines, and so render beautiful what might otherwise prove barren and unsightly. This would be an excellent position in which to grow a vine or two of the Niagara grape, as the building would afford it the protection it needs and the position on the south wall the necessary amount of sunshine and heat.

In renewing hotbeds and pits, the old manure in the bottom should be separated from the soil and thrown in a pile by itself, and may be used as a top dressing for bulb-beds, shrubbery, and the like.

The plant pit is another very useful adjunct to the garden, especially in the Middle and Southern States, but is of little use at the North, where it is only available for the wintering of tender roses, carnations, and the like—plants which require to be kept dry more than to be protected from frost.

It is possible, however, to make use of the pit for the raising of winter lettuce, radishes, and the like, when it can be constructed in connection with the cellar, and so receive heat from the furnace or other source. When this is undertaken, an excavation should be made on a south wall, reaching down to the cellar bottom and having an entrance into the cellar. The sash should slant sharply toward the south, and the frame should be of stone, cement, or brick construction, and if this can be built with a hollow wall, so much the better. Hollow cement tile furnishes a good, solid construction, or concrete may be built hollow by the use of cores. The sash should be provided with heavy wooden shutters and mats of straw or rugs to protect the pit in severe weather; these should be removed during the day whenever the weather permits. If the pit opens out of a furnace cellar and receives a good amount of sunshine, considerable growth will be made during the winter. The pit should be provided with shelves, which will permit of the placing of such plants as are wanted for immediate use close to the glass. Plants which are to be merely carried through the winter may rest on the floor of the pit or be placed midway between the top and floor.

In a mild climate a shallow pit may be built against a south-cellar wall and access gained to it through a cellar window. This is a most inexpensive form of pit and affords an excellent place for the growing of violets.

CHAPTER EIGHTEEN
THE GARDEN'S ENEMIES

The price of a good garden and orchard is a never-ceasing warfare on insect pests and plant-diseases.

But some will say, " What's the use of my keeping up the fight when my neighbour next door doesn't do anything, and insects and diseases of all kinds breed on his premises and then come over to mine? "

It is true that the work is made much more difficult without the co-operation of your neighbours, as it will have to be done continually and without much real satisfaction, but my advice is to keep up your efforts. Your neighbour may come to see his folly, but if he doesn't, laws will soon be enacted, I believe, compelling owners to spray and care for infected trees and shrubs.

Spraying merely frees us for the time being; it does not eradicate the pests entirely. If it did, we

THE VEGETABLE GARDEN

shouldn't have any pests, because, no matter how much behind the times a person might be, he would make one supreme effort, and spray, to rid his garden of bugs and disease. We must spray continually, and all our efforts will only keep the insects in check. This can be accomplished best by killing as many of the bugs as possible before they breed.

The various pests may be expected to appear about as follows:

APRIL.—Aphis or green plant-lice and asparagus beetle.

MAY.—Aphis, Colorado potato beetle, flea-beetle, cut-worms.

JUNE.—Cabbage worms, Harlequin or fire-bug, root maggot on cabbage and cauliflower, club root, corn ear-worm, striped beetle on cucumbers, melons, and squashes, onion maggot, thrips.

JULY.—Bean anthracnose, celery rust, squash bug, melon blight and mildew, tomato fruit worm.

AUGUST.—Asparagus rust, celery caterpillar, mildew on peas, potato blight, potato scab, squash borer.

The following is a list of the more common vegetables and the insects and plant diseases attacking them, with remedies or preventives:

Asparagus.—*Beetles.*—Keep beds closely cut in spring and protect the stalks with poison, preferably arsenate of lead.

Rust.—Spray thoroughly a few times in July and August with diluted Bordeaux. Set plants on good land, and keep them in vigorous condition.

Bean.—*Anthracnose.*—Spray with Bordeaux mixture when the first true leaf appears, making a second and third application when it is necessary to keep the foliage covered.

Bean Beetle.—Kill grubs on under side of leaves with kerosene emulsion (1 to 8) or spray with arsenate of lead.

Bean Weevil.—Fumigate beans for twenty-four hours in a tight vessel, using one tablespoonful of carbon bisulphide to the bushel.

Flea Beetles.—Spray with poisoned Bordeaux mixture.

Beet.—*Leaf Spot.*—Spray with Bordeaux mixture when four or five leaves have expanded, and repeat two or three times at intervals of ten to fourteen days.

Cut-worms.—Use poisoned baits, and prevent

attack by early fall ploughing, harrowing, or disking.

CABBAGE AND CAULIFLOWER.—*Aphis.*—Spray with kerosene emulsion, or a whale-oil-soap solution, when numerous, and repeat if necessary.

Cabbage Worm.—Spray with a poisoned resin-lime mixture, if plants have not headed; otherwise use hellebore or kerosene emulsion.

Club Root.—Large clubs or knobs on roots. Dig up and destroy all infested plants, and give soil a heavy dressing of lime. Never plant either of these vegetables on land known to be infected.

Cut-worms.—Protect stems with bands of paper or use poisoned bait.

Harlequin Cabbage Bug.—Sow mustard early as a catch crop and destroy the bugs thereon with kerosene, or resort to hand-picking.

Root Maggot.—Protect plants with paper collars, or wet the surrounding soil with emulsion composed of one pound of soap, one gallon of boiling water, and one pint of crude carbolic acid diluted with thirty parts of water.

CELERY.—*Blight.*—Make fortnightly applications of Bordeaux mixture until plants are one-half or two-thirds grown, then use an ammoniacal

THE GARDEN'S ENEMIES

copper carbonate solution every ten to fifteen days, if the weather is rainy.

Celery Worm.—A pea-green worm with black bands. Hand-pick and spray with Paris green or arsenate of lead.

CORN.—*Earworm.*—A small worm which eats out the tip of the ear. Poison them by dropping dry Paris green in the axils of the leaves when plants are young. Plough deeply in fall and leave the land rough, so that frost can work through it thoroughly.

CUCUMBER. — *Aphis.* — Spray with kerosene emulsion or whale-oil soap as soon as they are noticed.

Striped Beetle.—A small black- and white-striped beetle which is very active. Protect plants when young by screens, and dust them when wet with dew with ashes or lime. Spray with Bordeaux mixture containing arsenate of lead every two weeks to keep foliage well covered.

Squash Bug.—A dark-brown beetle which sucks the plant's juices. Hand-pick and destroy any eggs found on leaves. In the fall put down small boards or shingles, under which bugs will collect at night; gather and destroy.

THE VEGETABLE GARDEN

Blight or Mildew.—Leaves become spotted or covered with down. Spray every two weeks with Bordeaux mixture.

ONION.—*Blight.*—Spray with two-thirds strength Bordeaux mixture at ten-day intervals.

Maggot.—Wet the surrounding soil with carbolic-soap wash, or remove the soil about the plants in the morning, replacing at night, so as to allow some drying of soil about the maggots.

PEA.—*Aphis.*—Spray with kerosene emulsion, or a whale-oil-soap solution, when it is necessary.

Weevil.—Same as for bean weevil.

Mildew.—White growth on stems and leaves. Spray with Bordeaux mixture containing resin wash to make it stick.

POTATO.—*Colorado Beetle.*—Spray with Paris green or arsenate of lead every two weeks. To save time, add the poison to Bordeaux mixture when spraying for blight.

Flea Beetle.—Keep plants well covered with Bordeaux mixture.

Blight.—Spray every two weeks with Bordeaux mixture.

Scab.—Soak uncut tubers one and one-half hours in a solution of $\frac{1}{2}$ ounce of corrosive subli-

There is no use making a garden unless you propose to defend it against its enemies. The knapsack type of sprayer works well in large gardens. The small gardener will be delighted with the handy type of Aerospra, Jr.

Don't let the leaf chewing insects feast at your expense. Paris Green or Slug Shot are good remedies to keep on hand. The handy duster makes the work a pleasure

THE GARDEN'S ENEMIES

mate to 8 gallons of water, or for two hours in a solution of one pint of formaldehyde to 15 gallons of water.

Squash.—*Squash Borer.*—Slit infested stem, and destroy the borer, covering the injured part with earth. Employ early trap vines.

Squash Bug.—Trap bugs under shingles laid about vines, destroying them every morning, and crush egg clusters. See, also, Cucumber.

Sweet Potato.—*Black Rot.*—Select clean tubers, roll in sulphur, and, if possible, plant in soil free from infection.

Flea Beetles, Tortoise Beetles.— Dip young plants in arsenate of lead mixture, and spray ten days later, if necessary.

Tomato.—*Leaf Blight.*—Spray with Bordeaux mixture at seven- to ten-day intervals.

Flea Beetle.—Spray with poisoned Bordeaux mixture as needed.

Rot.—Treatment same as for leaf blight, though usually unsatisfactory.

Tomato Worm. — Hand-picking; spray with poison.

Other Vegetables.—*Cut-worms.*—Protect base of plant stems with strips of paper reaching just

THE VEGETABLE GARDEN

below the surface. Use poisoned bait, or dig out and destroy.

POISON FORMULAS

Many of the remedies advocated may be secured ready-made at the seed stores for use in the small garden. These ready-made mixtures are much more convenient for the amateur than the mixing of them from the raw materials. It is often necessary, however, to use considerable quantities and special combinations.

Combined Insecticides and Fungicides

POISONED BORDEAUX.—Mix 4 ounces of Paris green, or 1 pound of arsenate of lead with 50 gallons of Bordeaux mixture (see formula under Fungicides). This is the standard remedy for leaf-eating insects and fungous diseases.

Insecticides

PARIS GREEN.—Use 1 pound, with an equal weight of thoroughly slaked lime, in 100 to 300 gallons of water. Keep well stirred while spraying.

ARSENATE OF LEAD.—Use the prepared paste form, at the rate of about 1 pound to 50 gallons of

THE GARDEN'S ENEMIES

water, or it may be made by dissolving 11 ounces of acetate of lead (sugar of lead) in 4 quarts of water, in a wooden pail, and 4 ounces of arsenate of soda (50 per cent purity) in 2 quarts of water in another wooden pail. The process can be hastened by using warm water. Pour the solutions in from 25 to 50 gallons of water, mix, and the insecticide is ready for use.

ADHESIVE POISON.—Put 1 pint of fish oil, or any cheap animal oil except tallow, 5 pounds of resin, and 1 gallon of water in an iron kettle, and heat till the resin is softened, then add 1 pound of concentrated lye, in solution made as for hard soap; stir thoroughly, add 4 gallons of water, and boil about two hours, or until the mixture unites with cold water, making a clear amber-coloured liquid, and dilute to 5 gallons. Mix 1 gallon of this solution with 16 of water and three gallons of milk of lime, or thin whitewash; add thereto $\frac{1}{4}$ pound of Paris green or other arsenical poison. Recommended for spraying cabbage and other crops that have foliage to which it is difficult to make the insecticide adhere.

POISONED BAITS.—Dip fresh clover, lettuce, or other attractive leaves in strongly poisoned water

THE VEGETABLE GARDEN

and distribute in infested localities. Twenty pounds dry middlings and 1 pound of Paris green, well mixed, is an attractive bait. A mash composed of 1 pound of Paris green to 50 pounds of bran, and sweetened with cheap sugar or molasses, is very attractive to grasshoppers. Paris green 1 part, salt 2 parts, and horse droppings (preferably fresh) 35 to 40 parts by measure, thoroughly mixed with enough water to make a soft though not sloppy paste, is a valuable grasshopper poison.

KEROSENE EMULSION.—Dissolve $\frac{1}{2}$ pound of soap in 1 gallon of boiling water, add 2 gallons of kerosene, and force through a pump repeatedly for five to ten minutes; dilute four to twenty-five times before applying. In lime regions, where the water is hard, use a sour-milk emulsion, made by thoroughly mixing 2 gallons of kerosene and 1 gallon of milk, as described above.

WHALE-OIL-SOAP SOLUTION.—Apply at the rate of $1\frac{1}{2}$ to 2 pounds to a gallon of water in the winter, and for summer use employ at least 4 gallons of water to each pound of soap.

IVORY-SOAP SOLUTION.—Dissolve a five-cent cake in 8 gallons of water. Good for house plants.

HELLEBORE.—Mix thoroughly 1 ounce of fresh

THE GARDEN'S ENEMIES

white hellebore with 3 gallons of water. Use on fruits.

TOBACCO DUST.—This waste from tobacco factories may be used freely in trenches around trees with roots infested with aphids.

CARBOLIC-SOAP WASH.—Thin 1 gallon of soft soap with an equal amount of hot water, and stir in 1 pint of crude carbolic acid ($\frac{1}{2}$ pint refined) and allow this to set over night, then dilute with 8 gallons of water. Or dissolve 1 gallon of soft soap in 6 gallons of a saturated solution of washing soda. Add 1 pint of crude carbolic acid and mix thoroughly. Slake enough lime in 4 gallons of water so that a thick whitewash will result, then add $\frac{1}{2}$ pound of Paris green and mix the whole together. Recommended for borers.

Fungicides

NORMAL OR 1.6 PER CENT BORDEAUX MIXTURE.—Dissolve 6 pounds of copper sulphate, by hanging it in a bag of coarse cloth in an earthen or wooden vessel containing 4 to 6 gallons of water, and then dilute with 25 gallons. Slake 4 pounds of lime diluting to 25 gallons and mix by pouring the two solutions into a third vessel.

The amount of copper sulphate should be reduced to 4 pounds for peaches and Japanese plums, and some have used but 2 pounds each of copper sulphate and lime to 50 gallons, with excellent results. Employ the weaker formula whenever the normal proves too strong.

AMMONIACAL COPPER CARBONATE.—Make a paste of 5 ounces of copper carbonate with a little water, and dilute 3 pints of ammonia (26 Beaumé) with 7 or 8 volumes of water. Add the paste to the diluted ammonia, stirring till dissolved, and add enough water to make 45 gallons. Allow it to settle and use only the clear blue liquid. This mixture loses strength on standing.

POTASSIUM-SULPHIDE SOLUTION.—Dissolve ½ to 1 ounce of potassium sulphide (liver of sulphur) to 1 gallon of water.

COPPER-SULPHATE SOLUTION.—Dissolve 1 pound of copper sulphate (blue vitriol) in 15 to 25 gallons of water. Never apply this to the foliage. Use only before the buds break. For peaches and nectarines, dilute with 25 gallons of water.

FORMALIN.—Dilute 1 pound (1 pint) with 50 gallons of water, sprinkle on grain, stirring thoroughly and leave in piles for several hours for grain

THE GARDEN'S ENEMIES

smut. Use 1 pound to 30 gallons of water and soak seed potatoes therein for about 2 hours, for potato scab.

There are many kinds of apparatus for spraying, such as power-sprayers, barrel-pumps, bucket-sprayers, and hand-sprayers, and they usually come fitted with proper nozzles. Where the work must be done by one person, the air-pressure sprayers are the best, as the machine can be charged, and all attention can be directed to the spraying. The 5-gallon size is best for the small garden.

Another very good sprayer for the amateur with a small garden is a bucket spray-pump. These are the cheapest pumps on the market. Some sell for as low as two dollars, but I wouldn't advise any one's buying the cheapest. Pay from four to five dollars, and get a good one, with all the working parts of brass, which, with good care, will last a number of years. This style of sprayer comes with a short hose, which is convenient for spraying low shrubs and vegetables; but, if you have a few trees to spray, it will be necessary to buy an extra twenty-five feet of hose. To spray the tops of them, tie the nozzle on the end of a rake handle, and stand on a step-ladder to reach the highest parts.

CHAPTER NINETEEN
FALL WORK IN THE GARDEN

Fall work practically closes the year's work in the garden, while, at the same time, it may be said to be introductory and initiative to the beginning of another season's work, as it clears the way for the first operations of the spring, and, if thoroughly done, simplifies it in a marked degree.

The first thing in order will be to clear away all rubbish that may have accumulated during the summer, and pile it on the compost heap, or if it is of a character not likely to be infested with the larvi of insects, to use it as a winter mulch about the trunks of fruit trees, about the rhubarb rows, or as a winter protection for the asparagus bed. If, however, the rubbish be in the nature of weeds, in which seeds exist, the best course will be to rake it into a light, dry pile and burn it. The resulting ashes will be of benefit to the garden.

The presence of sod along fence rows and about

the roots of trees is objectionable, and the fall is a good time to get rid of it, as after the fall rains have thoroughly soaked the ground, it is easily lifted and may be used to protect the beds of tea-roses, wrapping a chunk of sod—grass-side out—about the roots of each plant, forming a cone, and securing it with a stout piece of binder twine if necessary. Or it may be piled in a heap, with alternating layers of cow manure, and left to decay until spring, when it may be used to enrich the rose or peony beds or other plants requiring fertilising. Again, it may be left where dug, simply turning it grass-side down about the trees or vines from which it was removed, until spring, when, if sufficiently decayed, it may be worked into the soil.

The fall is a good time in which to prepare for a very early crop of peas by trenching the ground where they are to be planted, filling in a generous quantity of well-rotted manure and placing the necessary amount of earth above this to receive the seed, leaving that portion which will be placed over the seed in a ridge along the trenches. The action of the frost will keep it loose and mellow, and as soon as the ground has dried sufficiently in the

THE VEGETABLE GARDEN

spring the seed may be gotten into the ground with the least possible delay and labour.

It is possible that at this season there will remain a number of cabbage and cauliflower plants, especially the latter, which have failed to make heads. These may be lifted and planted in coldframes, or even protected where they are by banking the earth about the stems and protecting the tops with straw, and used for very early planting in the spring. Or if a few rough boards can be run along one side of them where they stand to form a shelter from the west wind and a little litter of corn fodder thrown over them to form a shed, they will usually come through all right.

If a similar protection is given the parsley bed, using evergreen boughs, if procurable, for the shelter on the leaward side, parsley can usually be had all winter.

Every effort should be made at this season to get rid of all insect pests which hibernate in any form; a few hours spent in this work will be well repaid. The cut-worm, which is the first pest to appear and cause trouble in the spring, hibernates in the worm form usually and may be discovered along the edges of the sod land under boards and other rubbish which lie close to the ground; he does not go far in the earth at this time of year, and a light scraping of the surface of the ground will unearth him in numbers; wherever found, he should be killed at once. Most of the borers change into smooth, brown chrysalids in the fall, and are found in the ground not far from the surface. Fall ploughing and spading is of much benefit, as it destroys considerable numbers of these pests. The cabbage butterfly lays its eggs and hatches out the succulent green worm, which, arriving at an adult stage, spins itself a silken chrysalid which is transmitted into a hard, paper-like shell, which will be found attached to the underside of the window sills, house siding, and other favourable places, the worms sometimes travelling considerable distances to find favourable winter quarters, the shelter they require being of the slightest, a quarter of an inch of projecting wood seeming to meet all requirements.

The tomato worm enters the ground to a considerable depth before changing into the large brown chrysalid, with its curious-shaped handle, which is the case for its equally curious tongue. In studying these worms at close range, it was always one of the difficulties in their rearing to give them boxes of earth of sufficient depth to induce them to change at the right time. They would enter the earth and penetrate to the bottom and return again and again to the surface, each time more irritable and uneasy, until finally Nature proved too much for them and they were compelled to accept conditions as they found them. It is a very fascinating study—this of the moths and butterflies—when one can watch them through the four changes—winged creature, infinitesimal egg, the curious, often beautiful, worm, and its still more curious shell and cradle through which it braves the storm of winter as it waits for the resurrection of the spring. The worms lose much of their repulsiveness when studied at close range, and in captivity soon come to know one and to show none of the signs of irritation displayed by the wild worms, or the tame ones in the presence of strangers.

Many gardeners make a practice of hauling manure to the garden in the fall, that it may leach into the soil during the winter and be ready to turn under in the spring; this is of doubtful value, as much of the substance of the manure is lost. A better plan would be to pile the manure

FALL WORK IN THE GARDEN

under shelter, where it would be protected from the action of the elements, and to fork it over often during the winter to prevent heating, and then to draw it on the land early in spring while yet the ground is frozen enough to get on to it easily. In a small garden plot it is seldom, if ever, necessary to use much rough manure, and it will be well to fork out all the cornstalks and coarse material and pile them in a heap to burn, or better compost them, as they are nothing but a nuisance in a garden.

In February the wood ashes which may have accumulated during winter may be spread on the asparagus beds and along the rhubarb rows, and, if there are enough, about the fruit trees and berry bushes.

If one has a few choice fruit trees it will be time well spent to give them a coat of whitewash at the approach of severe weather and again at intervals during the winter, making at least three applications, the last to precede the cold waves of February and March, according to locality. This will protect the trees by preventing the absorption of sun heat and enable them to withstand the rigours of the winter.

THE VEGETABLE GARDEN

A heavy mulch about the roots of the fruit trees in any section where there is a light or no snowfall will be of the greatest benefit.

It is a good plan to place the manure directly on the ground in the fall or early winter under the trees; it is also an excellent time to secure it and so have it in readiness for early spring use, and if there is no convenient place in which to store it, it may still be engaged and its time of delivery fixed, always remembering that old manure is what is wanted and that that will be found at the bottom of the pile, and it should be clearly stipulated that this is what is to be delivered.

If any seeds have been saved from the garden, these should be sorted out and stored in properly labelled bags or boxes against the time they will be wanted in the spring. In addition to the label the packets should always bear the date of their saving, as seeds are often carried over from year to year, and, not being dated, quite old seeds, unfit for planting, often come to be used much to the hindrance and loss of the gardener. While seeds are little affected by frost, I prefer to store them in a dry, frost-proof place if possible, and it is especially important that they be kept out of the reach

FALL WORK IN THE GARDEN

of mice, which much enjoy a banquet of melon, squash, or pumpkin seeds and do not disdain less succulent morsels.

The long winter evenings and any stormy days which find one at leisure may profitably be spent in getting ready for spring work, by putting all the tools in first-class order, painting them when necessary, oiling and sharpening them to a working edge. Racks for tomatoes may be manufactured quickly and cheaply by using three or four stakes with pointed ends and a couple of iron or wooden barrel hoops. These are nailed to the top of the stakes and to a point nine or ten inches below and are set over the plants as soon as they begin to make growth. Boxes for covering the melon hills may also be prepared and the frame for the hotbeds, if one is not already supplied with that convenience. Stakes for marking rows of vegetables will be little work to prepare and will save time in the hurry of planting.

Many of the racks and trellises used about the garden during the summer will serve for another season if taken up and stored in a dry place over winter; especially will this be the case if any metal or wire parts are concerned. Fences and walks should be given attention and put in condition to stand the weather. Gates are prone to sag on the hinges and posts to work loose under the force of a winter's gale, and an hour's work in this portion of the yard may save a day's work during the busy time of spring.

And last, but not least, it will be a good plan to make a brief but orderly record of the season's work, noting down all failures and their cause, recording all new information which has been gained, such as the amount of time it requires for the various seeds to germinate, the length of time it takes for the different vegetables to come into bearing, the proportion of seed which germinated, the causes, as far as known, for any seed to fail to grow, the quality of the several varieties of vegetables, and any data as to better varieties grown in a neighbour's or market gardener's grounds.

All this data will be of value in starting the next season's garden, and will be always available and reliable, which is seldom the case where the memory alone takes charge of these items.

THE END

INDEX

Ammoniacal copper carbonate, 218
Anthracnose, 208, 209
Aphis, 208
Arsenate of lead, 214
Ashes, 38, 225
Asparagus, 154
   beetle, 208, 209
   forcing, 158

Bait, poisoned, 215
Bean, 75, 209
   varieties, 77
Beans, Lima, 77
Beetle, asparagus, 208, 209
   bean, 208, 209
   flea, 208, 209
   potato, 208, 212
   striped, 208, 211
Beets, 100, 167, 209
   best varieties, 101
Blight, celery, 210
   cucumber, 211
   melon, 208
   onion, 212
   potato, 208, 212
Bone, 30
Bordeaux mixture, 208, 214
Borer, 208

Cabbage, 84, 208, 210
   best. varieties, 86

Cabbage, to prevent cracking, 85
   worm, 85, 210
Carbolic soap wash, 217
Carbon bisulphide, 209
Carrots, 101, 167
Cauliflower, 86, 210
Celery, 137, 176
Chard, 171
Club root, 208
Coldframe, 179, 202
Compost heap, 220
Concrete, 185, 191
Copper carbonate, ammoniacal, 218
   sulphate solution, 218
Corn, 82
   varieties, 84
   ear-worm, 211
   salad, 140
Cress, upland, 139
   water, 139
Cucumber, 129
   varieties, 130
Cultivation, 51
   intensive methods, 19, 56
Cultivators, hand and wheel, 67
Cutworms, 55, 208, 209

Damping off, 200
Diseases, 207

INDEX

Egg plant, 94, 196
Endive, 140
Enemies, garden, 207

Fall work, 220
Fertilizer, 21-33
   amount to apply, 34, 35
Fire bug, 208
Flea beetle, 208, 209
Formalin, 218
Fungicides, 217

Garden, planning the, 15
   site of, 10
Gardening, economic value, 1-4

Harlequin bug, 208, 210
Hellebore, 216
Hoe, 62
   wheel, 63
Horse-radish, 162
Hotbed, 179
   manure for, 192, 193
Humus, 22

Insecticides, 212, 213, 214
Insects, 208, 212, 213
Irrigation, 13
Ivory soap, 216

Kale, 142
Kerosene emulsion, 216
Kohlrabi, 168

Leaf blight, 208, 213
   spot, 208
Lettuce, 142, 169
   varieties, 143

Lime, 36
Location of rows, 18

Maggot, 208, 210, 212
Manure, 192, 224
   green, 24, 25
Melon, 131
Mildew, 208, 212
Mulch, 50, 52, 226
Mustard, 151

Nitrogen, 27, 28

Okra, 91
Onion, 103
   exhibition types, 106
   maggot, 208-212
   transplanting, 105
   varieties, 106

Paris green, 214
Parsley, 164
Parsnip, 109
Peas, 89
   best varieties, 91
Pepper, 92
Phosphoric acid, 30
Plant protectors, 226
Plants, hardening of, 44
   protection for, 226
Poison, formulas, 214
   adhesive, 215
Poisoned bait, 215
Potash, 32
Potassium-sulphide, 218
Potatoes, 111
   storing, 173
Potato beetle, 208, 212
Protection, winter, 222
Pumpkins, 135

INDEX

Radishes, 116, 121, 169
   varieties, 121
Records, 228
Rhubarb, 160
   forcing, 161
Rust, asparagus, 208, 209
   celery, 208, 210

Salads, 136
   lettuce, 142
Salisfy, 121
Scratch weeders, 67
Seeds, sowing, 39
Soil testing, 37
Spade, 65
Spinach, 152, 170
Spraying, 217, 219
   apparatus, 68, 219
Squash, 134
   storage, 175
   bug, 211, 213
Start, how to really, 17
Storing vegetables, 172
Sweet potato, 213
Swiss chard, 171

Tankage, 31
Thrip, 208
Tobacco dust, 217
Tomato, 72, 196
   staking, 73
   varieties, 75
   rot, 213
   worm, 208, 213
Tools, 60
   for tilling, 65
Transplanting, 45
Trellis, 72
Trenching, 221
Turnips, 122, 168

Vitamines, 97

Water-cress, 139
Watermelon, 133
Weevil, 208, 209
Weeders, 66
Whale oil soap, 216
Wheel-hoe, 63
Whitewash on fruit trees, 225
Wood ashes, 38, 225